The BOOK of Blessings

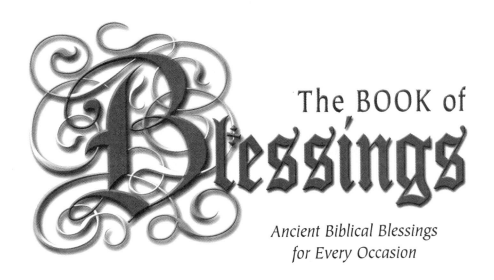

The BOOK of Blessings

*Ancient Biblical Blessings
for Every Occasion*

By John D. Garr, Ph.D., Th.D.

Bridge-Logos
Gainesville, Florida 32614

Bridge-Logos, Gainesville, FL 32614
Copyright © 2005 by John D. Garr

Printed in the United States of America.

05   1

Library of Congress Catalog Card Number: Pending
International Standard Book Number: 0-88270-954-2

Scripture quotations are from the Holy Bible, King James Version.

To my loving wife Pat
for blessing my life and
faithfully sharing my vision and ministry
these forty years.

Acknowledgements

I would like to express my appreciation for the blessing of shared insight that has come to me from friends and colleagues in ministry and in academia, including Dr. Karl D. Coke, president of Redirection Ministries in Charlotte, North Carolina, Dr. Doug Wheeler, president of Mended Wings Ministry in Bossier City, Louisiana, and Dr. Lynn Reddick, director of Open Church Ministries in Portal, Georgia. I am also grateful to Dwight A. Pryor, president of the Center for Judaic-Christian Studies in Dayton, Ohio, and Dr. Marvin R. Wilson, Professor of Biblical Studies at Gordon College in Wenham, Massachusetts, for their incisive and inspiring teaching on aspects of this subject. I am likewise deeply indebted to Judy Grehan for her careful examination of the manuscript and for her thoughtful suggestions for its improvement in both content and style.

$\mathcal{P}ref\ ace$

Huddled in a dimly lit corner of a subway car. Her eyes glazed over as she drifted in and out of conscious thought. Wheels rounding tight bends shrieked against steel rails in the darkened tunnel. The incessant clickety-clack, clickety-clack penetrated the night. But she was oblivious to all the rumble and roar.

A cold, damp draft from a crack in the door had painted her cheeks rosy red and had given a generous case of the sniffles to her Kleenex-muffled nose. Just as she nodded off in sleep, she was suddenly jolted into reality when a violent sneeze escaped from her lungs and exploded into the dank night air. *Aaah-choo!*

"Bless you!" "Bless you!" "Bless you!" *"Salud!"* *"Gesundheit!"* A chorus of reassuring blessings rose out of nowhere, resounding through the rocking train. Total strangers who moments before were not even there suddenly chimed in, offering exclamations of concern for one whose breath had been momentarily taken away.

This scene is repeated thousands, perhaps millions of times every day around the world. Is the exclamation, "Bless you!", a mere social convention? Is it only a hollow, meaningless custom? Or is there something in the human spirit that is designed by the Creator to bless others? Is there a biblical basis for our occasional, spontaneous outbursts of concern for others?

A Lost Legacy

There is, indeed, a rich biblical tradition of blessing that is virtually unknown and unused by the average Christian believer today. Most of the church is impoverished, robbed of this important aspect of their heritage as part of the believing community established in the faith of Jesus and the apostles. Millions of Christians have little or no knowledge of the blessing tradition that was foundational to the faith of the ancient Hebrews. Or if they do, they are convinced that blessing is reserved only for priests and ministers to do, and then, only in church ceremonies.

Very often, the only time that words of blessing are heard in the Christian community is at the conclusion of a worship service, and even then, it is received more as a sign that the exercise is finished than as a true blessing. The words of a benediction often signal only a yawn, an "amen," and a retreat into the secular world. Most worshipers are unaware of the far-reaching consequences of spoken words of blessing. As a result, they have been denied a rich and rewarding part of Christian faith and practice.

Back to the Bible!

In the ancient world of the Bible, people routinely blessed one another. They spoke blessings over homes, children, land, labors, travels, and resources of every sort. Blessings were used for greetings and for goodbyes. They were used to seal covenants and to settle conflicts. In following instructions laid out for them in Scripture, they did not allow a single day to go by without speaking words of blessing both for God and for others.

Even though blessings were so common in Bible times, they were certainly not meaningless. The ancients believed that something really happened when they spoke a blessing. They understood that the God they worshiped was a God of blessing. They were also convinced that the God of blessing had given them the power to bless, and they constantly used this gift that God had given them to bring his blessing into the lives of others.

When Christianity emerged from the Israelite community, the biblical practice of blessing in everyday life was soon lost. The Greco-Roman world had virtually no tradition of blessing, preferring only benedictions from temple priests and leaders of the people. It was preferable for new converts from this world to maintain their own cultural emphases than to adopt radically different practices from the Jewish culture of Jesus and his apostles.

A focus on the institutional church soon replaced the ancient emphases on family and community. The daily practice of blessing one another in home and village was replaced with formal worship led by an increasingly dominant clergy. Today, because of many generations of neglect, most Christians hardly think of spoken blessings at all.

If we are to understand and benefit from the divine blessing, we must go back to the Bible, not only in word, but also in deed. We must return to the biblical understanding of the blessing itself, of the one who blesses, and of the one who is blessed. We will never experience the fullness and richness of our Christian faith unless we first know the Hebrew Scriptures and the history and culture of the people of the Bible.

As a matter of fact, if we don't restore the Hebrew foundations of our Christian faith, we will continue to be victimized, robbed of the richness of our heritage. We will continue to miss out on things that God has given to us to draw us closer to him and to one another.

A Deep Human Longing

In a world filled with curses, there is a dire need for blessing. Lives pained by brokenness and loneliness are desperately longing for words of blessing. This is why there are so many books on blessing. Many of these promote pagan rituals that only lead people further from the divine truth about blessing. Christians will reject these counterfeit forms of blessings when they recognize that blessings are God's, and they must be done God's way.

It is high time that the church reexamined the biblically Hebraic blessing tradition that was repeatedly emphasized throughout the pages of the

Bible. It is time to restore this scriptural practice to the prominence that it occupied in the ancient biblical families and communities. It is time that believers in the God of Israel reclaim this teaching and its practical application for the health and well-being of all believers and of the church in general.

In this book, we will help you to understand how the tradition of blessing affected the lives of patriarchs and kings and of prophets and apostles in Bible days. You will learn how believers can still use words of affirmation on a daily basis to bring blessings to themselves and to others. You will be amazed at the number of biblical blessings that you can learn to speak into the lives of family and friends, and even total strangers, for that matter.

Get ready! You're going to be blessed, and you'll become a blessing!

Dr. John D. Garr

Contents

The God of Blessing

Many people today think of God as a harsh, distant being who is intent upon judging and punishing human beings. They instinctively know that they have failed to do what is right. They live in fear that somehow God can't wait to punish them for all the wrong things they have done.

The true image of the God of the Bible is just the opposite. The Almighty is always portrayed as a God of mercy, of loving kindness. "The Lord is good to all, and his tender mercies are over all his works" (Psalm 145:9). If God is anything, he is love. It is impossible to know God without knowing and manifesting love (1 John 4:8).

The apostle Paul captures God's blessing nature in these words: "Blessed be the God and Father of our Lord Jesus Christ, who has blessed us with every spiritual blessing in the heavenly places in Christ" (Ephesians 1:3, New International Version). God blesses his children with every blessing.

An Unbroken Record of Blessing

We know that God is a God of blessing today because it has always been a part of his nature to bless. The entire Bible is full of divine blessings upon those who approached God in faith and obedience. God has always been the God of blessing, and he will ever remain the one who blesses.

From the very beginning of time, God's original intent for all of creation was blessing. He blessed Adam and Eve. He provided a paradise for them filled with every blessing they could possibly have wanted. Of all the many blessings that God gave them, perhaps his greatest blessing was to create them in his own image and likeness.

God spoke a good word (benediction or blessing) to humanity immediately after he had created them: "Let them have dominion over ... the earth" (Genesis 1:26). God's blessing to humankind was that they would lead and maintain the earth in God's glory. Even after mankind fell into sin, God continued to speak this blessing of good news (the gospel) to succeeding generations: to Abraham (Galatians 3:8), to Israel (Hebrews 4:2-4), to the prophets (Daniel 7:18, 27), to the apostles (Luke 22:29-30), and to all believers (Matthew 25:34).

Even when Adam and Eve fell into sin, God's blessing continued to be manifest upon them even in what appeared to be the judgment of expulsion from the Garden of Eden. Their removal was a blessing in disguise, an act of God's mercy. It kept them from eating of the tree of life and living forever as sinners, eternally separated from God's presence. God's love even protected fallen man until the time would come for redemption and restoration through his son Jesus.

Without exception, God's universal intent for humanity, then, has been that of blessing. Even when judgment has been brought upon the wicked, it came as a result of their own evil, not God's intent. It has always been man's sin that has separated him from God. Man has withdrawn from his Creator into illusions of sin. God, however, has ever sought for those whom he could bless. The God of the Bible is the God of blessing.

The Breath of the Almighty

When God breathed into Adam's nostrils the breath of life, something amazing happened. More than oxygen filled Adam's lungs. Paul tells us that all Scripture is God-breathed (2 Timothy 3:16). When God's breath brought Adam to life, he also received a deposit of God's Word into the very essence of his being. As a result, the living words of God were in a measure written on humanity's heart from the beginning.

In order to make humanity in his image, God blessed Adam and Eve with the power of reason and placed in them a conscience as a spark of the divine that has since always drawn humanity to God. Even the descendants of Adam, who had no direct covenant with God, had God's Word in their hearts.

Listen to how Paul described God's amazing original blessing for humankind: "For when Gentiles who do not have the Law do instinctively the things of the Law, these, not having the Law, are a law to themselves, in that they show the work of the Law written in their hearts, their conscience bearing witness and their thoughts alternately accusing or else defending them" (Romans 2:14-15, New American Standard Bible).

God gave his Word—the very essence of what is "God-breathed,"—to Adam and to every subsequent human being. Since the beginning, God's instructions (often called "the law") have been written on human hearts so that their consciences have either condemned or excused them. In the words of Elihu of old, the breath of the Almighty gives man's spirit understanding (Job 32:8). This insight is the blessing that separates humanity from the animal world.

The Word of God that is implanted in the human heart generates faith for salvation and return to God. Faith comes by hearing God's Word (Romans 10:17). Because God's Word is written on man's heart, it is with the heart that man believes unto salvation (Romans 10:10). Creating faith is entirely God's activity. He alone speaks his Word to man and draws him to himself.

God's Imprint on Man's Heart

Blessing, then, is implanted into the very fiber of human life. God's likeness and image are stamped in the heart of every human being. His Word constantly speaks blessing into every life and warns against the curse of sin. Both the good and the bad in the earth are objects of God's blessings, for he causes the sun to shine on the evil and the good, and he sends the rain upon both the just and the unjust (Matthew 5:45). All human beings are the same; all are equal before their Maker. The only difference in the righteous is that they are saved from sin by God's grace.

When an echocardiogram is made of the human heart, it reveals a startling image that confirms this amazing biblical truth. It clearly shows that the tissues that separate the chambers of the heart are aligned in such a way as to form the Hebrew letter *shin*. Among the ancient people of the Bible and their descendants, the letter *shin* has been used as a symbol for God, for it is the first letter of *Shaddai* (the Almighty), one of the most significant names applied to God throughout the Bible.

Is this image a mere coincidence, or is it evidence that God has left the imprint of his name on the very heart of every human being who has ever lived on this earth? Do all of the more than six billion people living on this planet today bear the image of the God of the Bible written on their hearts? Is there a spark of the divine in all humans that ever draws them toward God and what they intuitively know is right and good? Does this imprint of the divine on the human heart give an innate inclination toward doing good even in the face of surrounding evil? Is there a blessing inclination in every human heart?

Though the heart of man is so deceitful and desperately wicked that only God can know it (Jeremiah 17:9), still the God of blessing has maintained a spark in men's hearts that becomes a torch of enlightenment through the word of faith. The human heart is one of the places where God has chosen to place his name, the signature that proves his ownership of all humanity. "The earth is the LORD's and all that it holds, the world

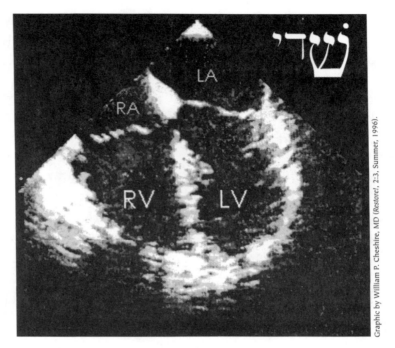

Graphic by William P. Cheshire, MD (*Restore!*, 2:3, Summer, 1996).

In the echocardiogram above, the Hebrew letter *shin* is clearly seen in the tissues that surround the chambers of the human heart. The letter *shin* is the universally recognized symbol for the divine name *Shaddai*, "The Almighty [God]" (seen at right above.)

and its inhabitants" (Psalm 24:1, JPS *Tanakh*, Hebrew Version). And, all that God possesses is the object of his lavish love poured out in blessing after blessing.

Original Blessing

Despite God's eternal commitment to bless mankind, the fall of Adam and Eve into sin has been viewed by most Christian teachers as the defining moment in the history of the human race. And, indeed, the Bible makes it clear that all men are slaves to sin (Romans 3:23; 5:12). King David lamented the human condition that had produced his unspeakable sin: "I was born with iniquity; with sin my mother conceived me" (Psalm 51:5). The Apostle Paul shared the pain of sin's addiction: "The good that I will to do I do not do: but the evil that I will not to do, that I practice" (Romans 7:19.). The record of human history is clear: "There is none righteous, no not one" (Romans 3:10).

Since God is the God of blessing, he was not content to leave man in his fallen state. While men have almost always been fixated on sin, God has been focused on blessing. His faithfulness to bless humankind was not blocked by sin. He simply further extended his tender mercy in terms that have never been nor can ever be fully understood. "For God so loved the world that he gave his only begotten Son, that whoever believes in him should not perish but have everlasting life" (John 3:16).

To ensure the fulfillment of his original blessing to humanity, God was manifest in the flesh. In the person of his Son, he overcame sin and offered himself as atonement for the sins of humanity. Now, all who come to faith in Jesus are delivered from the power of sin and its curse, and they enter fully into the blessing of the Father.

Humanity's liberation from sin, however, is nothing more than the completion of God's never-ending commitment to bless mankind. From the very beginning, his eternal plan provided for redemption through the sacrificed Lamb of God who takes away the sin of the world (John 1:29). Indeed, Jesus is the lamb slain from the foundation of the world (Revelation 13:8). Adam's fall was foreseen, and provision was made before the fall to fulfill the covenant and blessing. The life, death, and resurrection of Jesus merely provided the means by which the covenant and blessing that were originally intended could be fully restored to mankind. God, therefore, has never been fixated on man's sin; he has always been committed to man's blessing.

God is the God of blessing. He always has been, and he always will be. Jesus Christ is the same yesterday, today, and forever. He will never change; he will never compromise his covenant faithfulness that is ever manifest in the blessings he brings to his children.

God's Personal Blessing

The most beautiful blessing in the Bible is the one that God himself composed and dictated to Moses over three thousand years ago. This blessing says, "The LORD bless you and keep you. The LORD cause his face to shine upon you and be gracious unto you. The LORD turn his face toward you and give you peace" (Numbers 6:24-26).

This ancient blessing is so powerful that it has been known among biblical peoples simply as "The Blessing." What makes it so amazing is not that God spoke it once in history, but that God established a system to ensure that it would be pronounced upon all of the children of Israel forever. "The Blessing" has been called the *Aaronic Benediction* because God made

Aaron, the high priest, and his descendants responsible for speaking this blessing over the Israelites throughout all their generations.

When the temple was destroyed and the priesthood was dispersed nearly two thousand years ago, responsibility for speaking God's personal blessing upon the children transferred to the heads of families in Israel, while the descendants of the priests continued to make the blessing in corporate meetings. Jewish people have considered their homes to be temples in miniature (*mikdash me'at*); therefore, for centuries they have faithfully spoken God's blessing over their children in their small family sanctuaries.

Three Blessings in One

"The Blessing" is really three blessings in one, three complete sentences. Since there are three persons in God—Father, Son, and Holy Spirit—it is only fitting that there are three blessings in God's one personal blessing.

The **first blessing** says, "The LORD bless you and keep you." These words are from God the Father, and they reveal two things about his nature as Father: He is determined to bless and keep his children. The Father is the shepherd who guards Israel and all his children and blesses them with unlimited blessings.

The **second blessing** says, "The LORD cause his face to shine upon you and be gracious unto you." These words of benediction come from the Son of God who is the person who put a face on the Father so that when one saw Jesus, he saw the Father (John 14:9). Since "no man has seen God at any time," the "only begotten Son has revealed him" (John 1:18). The Son of God is "the radiance of God's glory and the exact representation of his being" (Hebrews 1:3), for God caused his glory to shine in the face of Jesus Christ (2 Corinthians 4:6). It is Jesus who causes the face of God to shine upon humanity, and it is he who uniquely brings God's grace into men's lives, for "grace and truth came through Jesus Christ" (John 1:17).

The **third blessing** says, "The LORD turn his face toward you and give you peace." These words are from the Holy Spirit, the person of God who confronts humanity with God's grace and is the agent of God's peace, who gives a peace that passes understanding (Philippians 4:7).

Placing the Divine Name

When God dictated his personal blessing to Moses, he concluded by saying that when the blessing was spoken over the children of Israel, God's own personal name would be placed upon them and he would bless them. While there are many names that men have used to describe God, there is only one name that God chose for himself, the name YHWH (Yahweh). God's personal name means, "I am that I am" or "I will be what I will be," or simply, "I will be."

When "The Blessing" is spoken, God's name (which is no longer pronounced but is represented in English by "The Lord") is repeated three times, once in each of the three blessings in "The Blessing." In order to fulfill God's statement, "They will put my name upon the children of Israel," the priests also would also literally write God's name in Hebrew either on the forehead or in the right hand of the worshiper.

What a powerful image! Who would not want God's name to be written in his forehead? The very last book of the New Testament speaks of those who have "the Father's name written in their foreheads" (Revelation 14:1). Is it possible that by speaking the words of God's Blessing upon our children or over our congregations, we can be placing God's name on them?

Restoring Our Hebrew Legacy

"The Blessing" has no magical powers. After all, it was God, not the priests, who blessed. God said, "*I* will bless them." The Jewish people of history have always understood that only God can bless. Men can only serve as instruments through which God can bless.

The divine blessing, however, is not just a mere ceremonial formality. And it is not optional. It is God's command that his children be blessed throughout all their generations with the specific benediction that he formed and dictated to Moses. This threefold blessing is powerful and eternal. It is the generationally enduring promise of divine favor and all that it provides. It is the very personal blessing for even the lowest of human beings from the exalted Ruler of the universe.

Why would this blessing be so neglected among Christians when it has always been so important among the Jews? Perhaps in their rush to separate themselves from the Jewish community of history, the Christians left behind a great part of the Hebrew legacy that was foundational to the faith of Jesus and the apostles.

There are many wonderful and beautiful benedictions in the Holy Scriptures, including the New Testament. These can and should be repeated over congregations and individuals by those whom God has ordained as leaders in the community of faith. This should not, however, be done to the neglect of the one Blessing that God himself composed and commanded to be spoken upon all of his children forever.

The first place where this Hebrew legacy should be recovered is in the Christian home, where the parents should imitate their Jewish counterparts by blessing their own children with God's blessing. Secondly, when

God's Personal Blessing

The Lord bless you and keep you.

The Lord cause his face to shine upon you

and be gracious unto you.

The Lord turn his face toward you and give you peace.

יְבָרֶכְךָ יהוה וְיִשְׁמְרֶךָ

יָאֵר יהוה פָּנָיו אֵלֶיךָ וִיחֻנֶּךָ

יִשָּׂא יהוה פָּנָיו אֵלֶיךָ וְיָשֵׂם לְךָ שָׁלוֹם

Christians assemble for corporate worship, their leaders should remember God's commandment and speak his words of blessing over them collectively.

When this action is carried out in obedience to God's instructions, God makes this absolute promise: "I *will* bless them." Is there any doubt that God's Word works? When we do what he says, we reap the benefits. In this case, Christian lives would be much more blessed if they would give and receive God's blessing in home and congregation.

Blessing and Being Blessed

God's blessing nature was clearly manifest four thousand years ago in the life of one man. Abraham was chosen by God to be the first Hebrew. He was the object of God's covenant and blessing, and he became the channel through which God would bless "all the families of the earth." Paul even describes this ancient patriarch as "the father of us all" (Romans 4:16).

In Abraham, an eternal principle of blessing was established: God lavishes his blessings on his children so that they can, in turn, bless others. Listen to God's promise to Abraham: "I will bless you and make your name great, and you will be a blessing" (Genesis 12:2). God was so intent upon blessing Abraham that he swore an oath by his own name, saying, "Surely blessing I will bless you" (Hebrews 6:13-15), and "in you shall all the families of the earth be blessed" (Genesis 12:3).

God brought both covenant and blessing first to Abraham and then through him to the entire world. Abraham was a man of pure faith and faithfulness. He believed God. As a result, God made an everlasting covenant with him. God's blessing was the product of his covenant. Both the covenant and the blessing of Abraham were extended to the entire world through Jesus.

God did not bless Abraham just for his own personal benefit. God's blessing was given first to Abraham, then to his children, and finally to all the nations of the world. God's immediate intention was to bless the man of faith. God's final objective was to bless all those who would imitate the life of faith that Abraham lived.

God's blessing for Abraham was to become a dynamic model to the nations. God would use one whom he had blessed to become a channel of blessing for all men. God's blessing for the Abrahamic family was not just for their own benefit. It was not a scheme to develop a super race to dominate the world. God's covenant with Abraham and his descendants was for the purpose of serving the world with enlightenment and blessing. Abraham's blessing was a blessing to bless.

God's concern for blessing has always been the same, from the beginning to the end. He blessed humanity from the moment of creation, he continues to bless humanity now, and his final act for humanity will be blessing. And he has always blessed the ones he has chosen so they could bless all of his children.

Children of Abraham

All those who have come to faith in Jesus as Lord and Savior have become Abraham's children. "If you belong to Christ, then you are Abraham's descendants, heirs according to promise" (Galatians 3:29) God's promises and blessings for Abraham were not only for his physical descendants;

they were intended also for his spiritual descendants. Just like Father Abraham, then, Christians then are blessed of God in order to bless others.

Jesus declared that those who are the children of Abraham will do the works of Abraham (John 8:39). If Abraham is our father, then we will manifest the life of faith. When we do, we will find ourselves the object of God's blessing. Then, we will become channels of God's blessing to others. We will even become God's blessing-bearers to the nations.

Because Abraham had been appointed by God to be the channel of blessing to all the families of the earth, he often found himself engaged in prophetic intercession, imploring God's blessing in the lives of others. This he did for Lot (Genesis 13:8), for Ishmael (Genesis 17:18), and even for Sodom and Gomorrah (Genesis 18:22-33).

Christians today who are of Abrahamic faith will be more concerned for God's blessings for others than they are for themselves. They will be active intercessors, praying that God's blessings will come to all the people of the earth. They will begin by blessing their own families, then by blessing their neighbors and friends, then by blessing their communities and nations, and finally by blessing the world.

The Christian's blessing will not even be limited to family, friends, and loved ones. It will even be extended to enemies. Just like Abraham sought God's blessing on Sodom, they will obey the command of Jesus: "Love your enemies, bless those who curse you, do good to those who hate you, and pray for those who spitefully use you and persecute you" (Matthew 5:44).

Blessing and Grace

God is the source of all blessing, and the means by which blessing is conveyed is grace. Nothing that men can do will ever merit God's favor. Grace and the blessing it brings are the outpourings of God's love. God's determination to love and bless is unrelenting and can never be suppressed or abandoned.

In the New Testament, the word for grace is *charis* in Greek, which corresponds to *chen* in Hebrew, meaning "favor, grace, charm, elegance, or acceptance." It is also implied in the Hebrew word *chesed*, which means, "tender mercy or loving kindness." Grace, then, is the focus of blessing. "Grace be unto you," was a common greeting, as well as a benediction from the apostles (Romans 1:7; 16:24).

Man's very salvation is based upon God's grace: "For by grace are you saved through faith" (Ephesians 2:8). This grace is superabundant: "Where sin does abound, grace does much more abound" (Romans 5:20). When sin entered in, God's grace and its resultant blessing were not diminished. God merely expanded the range of his grace to account for man's disobedience and to provide a means of ensuring his blessing to all.

The Circle of Blessing

The model of blessing that God first applied to Abraham is clearly demonstrated in the New Testament. God blessed Abraham so he could be a blessing. Likewise, God still blesses all believers so they can bless others, who in turn bless God with thanksgiving and praise.

Blessing is given by God directly to men in the form of his grace (*charis* in Greek). Then, the grace and blessing are transferred to others through the gifts (*charismata* in Greek) that God has given to men. Notice the *charis* (grace) in the *charis-mata* (gifts) that are described in Romans 12 and 1 Corinthians 12.

The gift of grace blesses the one who receives it, and it empowers him to bless others. Paul observes that all believers have gifts that differ "according to the grace [*charis*]" that is given to them (Romans 12:6). Just like Father Abraham, Christians extend God's blessing laterally into the lives of others.

God's blessing, then, is given so that the person who is divinely blessed may, in turn, be a blessing to someone else. In order to bless others, one must become a channel through which God's blessing can flow. The grace

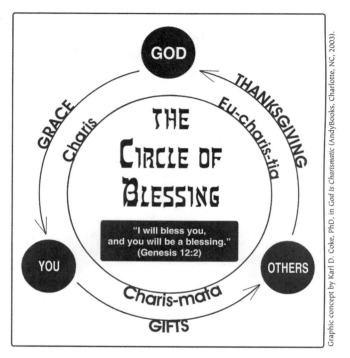

Graphic concept by Karl D. Coke, PhD, in *God Is Charismatic* (AndyBooks, Charlotte, NC, 2003).

The blessing of God's grace (*charis*) that is given to you is conveyed laterally to others by God's gifts (*charis-mata*) in your life. Both you and they then return the blessing to God in the form of thanksgiving (*eu-charis-tia*), completing the Circle of Blessing.

that is delivered vertically from God is channeled horizontally into the lives of others.

Recognizing God as the only source of all blessing promotes humility and the understanding that we cannot control the capacity to bless. At the same time, it also enables us to become highly available as channels of divine blessing. Those Christians who are the children of Abraham through faith are blessed of God in order to be God's blessing-bearers to others.

The beauty of this experience is that the grace and blessing never end either with the one who is bestowing the blessing or with the one who is receiving the blessing. Through thanksgiving (*eucharistia* in Greek), the grace and blessing are returned to God who gave them. Observe the *charis* (grace) in *eu-charis-tia* (thanksgiving). Those who are blessed either directly by God or indirectly through chosen and blessed vessels give praise to God. By giving thanks to him, the grace and blessing come full circle. The blessing that comes from God returns to God as praise.

This is why Paul said, "In everything give thanks [*eucharistia*], for this is the will of God in Christ Jesus concerning you" (1 Thessalonians 5:18). It is why David said, "I will bless the LORD at all times; his praise shall continually be in my mouth" (Psalm 34:1). The ancient Hebrew people understood that God was the source of all blessing. That is why they always blessed him with the voice of thanksgiving.

Blessing Reciprocity

It is impossible for a believer to bless someone else without being blessed in return. The divine energy of blessing is reflected from the one who is blessed and returns to the blesser. In like manner, blessings can have continuing impact on many others over long periods of time. A blessing for one can become a generational blessing.

God's blessing can never be bottled up. The word of benediction is so powerful that it produces a chain reaction of blessing. This is a part of the divine law of reciprocity: you receive what you give and in the same proportion in which you give. It is impossible to bless without being blessed.

Seven Reasons
Why You Should Bless

1 *You fulfill the instructions in the Word of God for blessing.*

2 *You establish and promote a culture and lifestyle of blessing.*

3 *You maintain a positive "Good News" mindset by blessing.*

4 *You manifest the gifts of the Holy Spirit through blessing.*

5 *You confirm your dependence on God as your source.*

6 *You reinforce to yourself and to others that God's Word works.*

7 *You are always blessed even more when you bless others.*

God's blessing is imparted to those who open their hearts to his grace. In turn, these humble souls who have qualified themselves as instruments of God's grace become channels through which the grace of blessing flows to others. Like Father Abraham, we do not consume the grace into ourselves. We always release it both to men and to God. We are blessed of God with a view toward blessing others. God expects it, and so do we. We learn to love as Christ did in self-sacrificing service that goes beyond human reason. In blessing others, we are blessed.

Family Blessings

he first place where God's blessings should be pronounced is in the home. For thousands of years this has been the case in Hebrew and Jewish homes. God's first promise to Abraham was this: "In you all the families of the earth shall be blessed" (Genesis 12:3). The Jewish people and their faith have survived centuries of unrelenting persecution solely because of the importance attached to the home as the locus for spiritual development. Their temple was destroyed, and countless synagogues have been burned. The Jewish home has remained the bedrock of the social and spiritual community.

The Hebrew people highly valued their families and maintained respect for parents, spouses, and children. The family was the unit for nurturing and strengthening individuals. Both husbands and wives profited from the balance of their covenant relationship. Children were nurtured in the security of a stable, loving, and blessed environment.

Christianity, on the other hand, has focused so much of its social and spiritual life on its corporate worship experience that, by default, it has neglected the importance of worship and other spiritual exercises in the home. This is particularly true of blessing. If words of blessing or benediction are given in Christian circles, they are generally reserved for the clergy. Most Christian parents have never stopped to think how important their homes are as places for worship, study of God's Word, and blessing.

A Sanctuary of Blessing

The home is not merely a social convention: it is a holy place, a sanctuary of blessing. In Jewish tradition, every home already contains an altar: the table. God's altar is called a table by Malachi (l:7, 12) and by Paul (1 Corinthians 10:21). If God's altar is a table, then the family table can be an altar. The table, then, is more than a piece of furniture for dispensing food. It is a focal point of the sanctuary where the family can gather for prayer, for fellowship, study of God's Word, and for blessing.

If you think that blessing is something that only priests or ministers can do, then consider the case of King David. He was not a priest; however, he often led Israel in worship. The Psalms are his offerings of praise and worship to God, songs that he sang to honor the Most High. On one occasion, David even led all of Israel in a spontaneous outburst of praise in which he "danced before the LORD with all his might" (2 Samuel 6:14).

This was the time when David was moving the Ark of the Covenant to Jerusalem. David believed in corporate worship, and he led Israel in a spectacular demonstration of praise. Listen to the focus of David's attention at the end of this public worship experience: "All the people went to their homes. And David returned home *to bless his household*" (2 Samuel 6:20, emphasis mine). Even though there were priests in Israel who were commissioned to bless the children of Israel, and even though he was the king of Israel, David remembered that it was his responsibility as the leader of his household to bless his family in the sanctuary of their home!

What the ancient priests did in the temple, you can do in your home. You can pray, teach the Bible, offer sacrifices of praise and thanksgiving, and bless your family. What King David did in his home, you can do in yours. And God has made it easy for you. The blessings are all in the Bible. You just can't go wrong using the inspired blessings in God's Word.

How often should you bless your children? In Jewish tradition, all family blessings are given at least once each week (on the Sabbath). This is a special time when the family gathers around the table in the sanctuary of the home, shutting out everything else. It is a time that helps everyone understand the things that are really important in life: God and family.

You can profit from incorporating this Jewish tradition into your Christian home. Set a time once a week to gather your family around the family altar (the table). Share food, fellowship, prayer, Bible reading, and family blessings. Husbands, bless your wives. Wives bless your husbands. Parents bless your children. And let everyone bless God!

Blessing by Faith

When Christians think of faith, they envision moving mountains, or they remember the astonishing miracles that are recorded in the Bible. "Now faith is the substance of things hoped for, the evidence of things not seen," they recall from Hebrews 11:1, and they are uplifted by accounts of saints translated, floods escaped, seas parted, and walls flattened. The Bible's "Faith Chapter" speaks of all of these miracles and more that were accomplished by faith.

In the midst of these accounts of astounding miracles, however, are two stories of faith that somehow don't measure up to our images of biblical faith: "By faith Isaac blessed Jacob and Esau in regard to their future. By faith Jacob, when he was dying, blessed each of Joseph's sons, and worshiped as he leaned on the top of his staff" (Hebrews 11:20-21).

Could blessing children in the home be an exercise of faith that is on a par with stopping the mouth of lions? Did Jesus perform as great a miracle when "he took the children in his arms, put his hands on them, and blessed them" (Mark 10:16) as when he said to the raging sea, "Peace, be still" (Mark 4:39)?

Blessing after Blessing

In the Bible, you will find numerous blessings for God (words of praise and thanksgiving). In Jewish tradition, there are numerous blessings for God that can be spoken so that God is praised at lease one hundred times each day. In the Bible, you will also find blessings for husbands, for wives, for sons, for daughters, for friends, and for strangers. You will find blessings for special occasions: for family meals, for holidays, for births, for weddings, for rites of passage, for graduations, for bereavement. There is a blessing for virtually everything.

How do you do it? It's really simple. Take someone's hand or lay your hand on them respectfully. Look into their eyes. Then speak the words of biblical blessings or create your own blessing from your heart. Don't worry about how "professional" you sound. Your heart should be talking, not your brain! Affirm the good that you recognize in the person you bless and speak the hope of your heart for them. As a child of God, you are authorized to speak these words: "The blessing of the LORD be upon you. We bless you in the name of the LORD" (Psalm 129:8).

There's nothing stopping you. Just do it.

Blessing Your Wife

Blessing your wife is important for your entire family: for you, for your wife, and for your children. You cannot speak the words of God's blessing over your wife if the words are not sincere and from your heart. Your wife will be blessed and esteemed both in her own eyes and yours. Finally, your children will see that you value and honor their mother, which builds their esteem for her and reinforces the feeling of the safety and stability of their home. You should bless your wife in the presence of your children during your weekly family time.

The blessing that the Bible gives for wives is found in Proverbs 31:10-31. This blessing, taught to King Lemuel (probably Solomon) by his mother, is even called a "prophecy" (Proverbs 31:1). According to Jewish tradition, Abraham spoke these words of blessing over his wife Sarah, and the prophetic words continued to be repeated generation after generation over the wives of his descendants. In some Jewish communities, husbands sing this entire scriptural blessing to their wives each Sabbath evening.

You may use all or parts of this blessing:

"What a rare find is a capable wife! Her worth is far beyond that of rubies. Her husband puts his confidence in her and lacks no good thing. She is good to him all the days of her life. She looks for wool and flax and sets her hand to them with a will. She is like a merchant fleet, bringing her food from afar. She rises while it is still night, and supplies provisions for her household, the daily fare of her maids. She sets her mind on an estate and acquires it. She plants a vineyard by her own labors. She girds herself with strength and performs her tasks with vigor. She sees that her business thrives. Her lamp never goes out at night. She sets her hand to the distaff; her fingers work the spindle. She gives generously to the poor; her hands are stretched out to the needy. She is not worried for her household because of snow, for her whole household is dressed in crimson. She makes covers for herself; her clothing is linen and purple. Her husband is prominent in the gates, as he sits among the elders of the land. She makes cloth and sells it, and offers a girdle to the merchant. She is clothed with strength and splendor. She looks to the future cheerfully. Her mouth is full of wisdom, her tongue with kindly teaching. She oversees the activities of her household and never eats the bread of idleness. Her children declare her happy. Her husband praises her, 'Many women have done well, but you surpass them all.' Grace is deceptive. Beauty is illusory. It is for her fear of the Lord that a woman is to be praised. Extol her for the fruit of her hand, and let her works praise her in the gates" (Jewish Publication Society *Tanakh*, a Hebrew translation).

A Blessing for Your Wife

What a rare find is a capable wife! Her worth is far beyond that of rubies. Her husband puts his confidence in her and lacks no good thing. She is good to him, never bad, all the days of her life … She gives generously to the poor; her hands are stretched out to the needy … Her husband is prominent in the gates, as he sits among the elders of the land … She looks to the future cheerfully. Her mouth is full of wisdom, her tongue with kindly teaching. She oversees the activities of her household and never eats the bread of idleness. Her children declare her happy. Her husband praises her, "Many women have done well, but you surpass them all." It is for her fear of the Lord that a woman is to be praised. Extol her for the fruit of her hand, and let her works praise her in the gates. In finding you, my wife, I have found happiness, and I have won the favor of the Lord.

You may want to add these words: "He who finds a wife has found happiness and has won the favor of the Lᴏʀᴅ" (Proverbs 18:22).

Blessing Your Husband

Blessing your husband is important for your entire family: for you, for your husband, and for your children. You cannot speak the words of God's blessing over your husband if the words are not sincere and from your heart. Your husband will be blessed and esteemed in both his own eyes, as well as in yours. Finally, your children will see that you value and honor their father, which builds their esteem for him and reinforces the feeling of the safety and stability of their home.

Though it is not generally the tradition in most Jewish homes for the wife to bless the husband, there is a wonderful biblical blessing that virtually mirrors the blessing that Proverbs 31 outlines for wives. It is found in Psalm 122:1-10: "Praise the Lᴏʀᴅ! Blessed *is* the man who fears the Lᴏʀᴅ, who delights greatly in his commandments. His descendants will be mighty

A Blessing for Your Husband

Praise the LORD! Blessed is the man who fears the LORD, who delights greatly in his commandments. His descendants will be mighty on earth; the generation of the upright will be blessed. Wealth and riches will be in his house, and his righteousness endures forever. Unto the upright there arises light in the darkness; he is gracious, and full of compassion, and righteous. A good man deals graciously and lends; he will guide his affairs with discretion. Surely he will never be shaken; the righteous will be in everlasting remembrance. He will not be afraid of evil tidings; his heart is steadfast, trusting in the LORD. His heart is established; he will not be afraid, until he sees his desire upon his enemies. He has dispersed abroad, he has given to the poor; his righteousness endures forever; his horn will be exalted with honor.

on earth; the generation of the upright will be blessed. Wealth and riches will be in his house, and his righteousness endures forever. Unto the upright there arises light in the darkness; he is gracious, and full of compassion, and righteous. A good man deals graciously and lends; he will guide his affairs with discretion. Surely he will never be shaken; the righteous will be in everlasting remembrance. He will not be afraid of evil tidings; his heart is steadfast, trusting in the LORD. His heart *is* established; he will not be afraid. He has dispersed abroad, he has given to the poor; his righteousness endures forever; his horn will be exalted with honor."

Blessing Your Children

"And [Jesus] took the children in his arms, put his hands on them and blessed them" (Mark 10:16). One would think that this one sentence in the Bible would be enough to impress upon all Christians the importance of blessing children. For Jesus, however, this was much more than a casual, spontaneous act of compassion and love. It represented a rich and foundational part of his heritage as a Jew among his Israelite family and community.

For thousands of years, the Hebrew people have regularly blessed their children, usually on a weekly basis. From the time that Jewish children are babes in arms, their parents take full advantage of their weekly Sabbath family time to lay their hands on each one of their children individually and speak God's blessing into their lives. As this blessing scenario continues into adolescence and beyond, Jewish children simply grow up feeling blessed. Is it any wonder, then, that such a large number of Jewish people are so successful in life?

Two of the earliest patriarchs of the Israelite community were recognized in the New Testament "Faith Hall of Fame" simply because of the blessing they pronounced upon their children. Both Isaac and Jacob are said to have blessed their children "by faith" (Hebrews 11:20-21). Joseph actually brought his sons to their grandfather's deathbed so the hands that had wrestled with the Lord could be placed upon their heads, and they could receive a blessing in the same manner in which the patriarch had been blessed of the angel at Peniel.

King David retreated into the sanctuary of his own home "to bless his household" immediately after he had led all of Israel in celebrating the return of the Ark of the Covenant (2 Samuel 6:20). Is there any leader in either civil or religious circles who has a job more important than blessing his own children?

Hands of Blessing

It is no coincidence that Jesus "put his hands" on the children when he blessed them. In our modern world, putting one's hands on a child's head may seem quaint or outdated, but in Bible days, it was the norm.

The Hebrew people believed that something actually happened when they laid their hands on their children. And their children believed it, too! All we have to do is to remember the length to which Jacob and his mother went to have Isaac's hands of blessing laid on Jacob's head. It is for this reason that Jewish children to this day are taught from a tender age to approach their fathers with their heads inclined to receive a blessing.

Is there magic in placing one's hands on another? No, but something does happen. In other examples of the Hebraic practice of "laying on of hands," authority, anointing, healing, and blessing were transferred. Joshua received an element of Moses' authority when the prophet laid his hands on him (Numbers 27:18-23). Timothy received a spiritual anointing when the elders laid their hands on him (1 Timothy 4:14).

The Creative Words of Blessing

Words have amazing power! They create, either for good or for evil. Negative statements foster negativity and produce undesirable results. Reinforcement from positive words generates optimism and promotes beneficial outcomes.

This is all the more true of the Word of God. It is alive and powerful (Hebrews 4:12). It is creative, the means by which everything that exists came into being (Hebrews 11:3). The Word also sustains all creation (Hebrews 1:3). The Word works!

The words of blessing, then, are powerful, especially when they are the words spoken by God himself. When we speak God's words over our children, something dynamic happens. Children hear the Word. The Word generates faith unto salvation. Positive words of blessing generate positive actions in children's lives. Impartation of blessing creates an environment of positive expectation and produces positive results. God simply honors his Word.

Nurturing in God's Instruction

Children need unconditional love and support. They need positive reinforcement. On a purely emotional level regular blessing provides both. On a spiritual level, however, much more is accomplished when children are blessed by their parents. They are nurtured in God's instruction. The Word of God becomes real to them, not just some distant myth or legend. They actually experience for themselves what happened in Bible days.

God knew what he was doing when he commanded that his blessing be placed on the children of Israel throughout all their generations. Jesus was simply doing what he had seen the Father do when he took the children in his arms, laid his hands on them, and blessed them. Do you want to be like Christ, a Christian indeed? Go and do likewise!

Blessing Your Son

In the biblical Jewish tradition, it is proper to bless your sons in this manner: Begin by laying your hand on his head and speaking the words that the Lord commanded the Israelites to say over their sons (Numbers 6:23): "The Lord bless you and keep you. The LORD cause his face to shine upon you and be gracious unto you. The LORD turn his face toward you and give you peace."

Next, you can speak a personal blessing over your son, expressing your own desires for his success and happiness. This is in keeping with the tradition of Jacob who blessed his twelve sons individually, "giving each the blessing appropriate to him" (Genesis 49:28).

You may also want to choose from among the blessings that Moses gave to the Twelve Tribes of Israel (Deuteronomy 33) those blessings that would be appropriate for your son:

"May you live long and abundantly before the Lord" [Reuben].

"May the Lord strengthen your hands and be a help to you whenever you call" [Judah].

"May God bless all your skills and be pleased the works of your hands" [Levi].

"May you be beloved of the Lord and be protected by him" [Benjamin].

"May the Lord bless your land with all the precious gifts of heaven and earth, that you may give a great inheritance to your children" [Joseph for Ephraim and Manasseh].

"May God bless your works in the world, that you may draw others to God's mountain" [Zebulun].

"May God bless your home, that your sacrifices may end in abundance, and your house be filled with his treasures" [Issachar].

"May God choose the leader's portion for you, that you may carry out the Lord's righteous will in the land." [Gad].

"May you be ever like a young lion, protecting your family and defending justice for your people" [Dan].

"May you always be abounding in the favor of the Lord and in his blessings" [Naphtali].

"May you be favored of your brothers and sisters, and may your strength never fail you to the end of your days" [Asher].

You may also add these charges: "May your mouth speak with wisdom. May your heart meditate with reverence. May your hands do the work

A Blessing for Your Son

The Lord bless you and keep you. The Lord cause his face to shine upon you and be gracious unto you. The Lord turn his face toward you and give you peace.

(Speak a personal blessing over your son.)

May your mouth speak with wisdom. May your heart meditate with reverence. May your hands do the work that God has given you. May your feet hasten to follow the path that God has laid out for your life. May the Lord's full will for you be accomplished.

May the Spirit of the Lord, the spirit of wisdom and understanding, the spirit of counsel and power, the spirit of knowledge and the fear of the Lord be upon you.

May the grace of our Lord Jesus Christ, the love of God, and the fellowship of the Holy Spirit be upon you both now and forever. Amen.

that God has given you. May your feet hasten to follow the path that God has laid out for your life."

You may then want to invoke the seven-fold Spirit of God upon your son: "May the Spirit of the LORD, the spirit of wisdom and understanding, the spirit of counsel and power, the spirit of knowledge and the fear of the LORD be upon you" (cf. Isaiah 11:2).

Finally, you may add this New Covenant benediction: "May the grace of our LORD Jesus Christ, the love of God, and the fellowship of the Holy Spirit be upon you both now and forever. Amen."

Blessing Your Daughter

Jewish parents bless their daughters each week on their Sabbath by first invoking the words of blessing that the Israelites placed upon Ruth: "The LORD make you like Rachel and Leah" (Ruth 4:11), for it was these two women who "together built the house of Israel." You may use this blessing or say, "May the LORD make you like Sarah and Rebecca, like Rachel and

Leah who together built the house of Israel. May your entire life be fruitful and may the Lord's full will for you be accomplished in your life."

Next, you will want to speak God's personal blessing over your daughter: "The Lord bless you and keep you. The Lord cause his face to shine upon you and be gracious unto you. The Lord turn his face toward you and give you peace."

Then, you can speak a personal blessing expressing your own desires for your daughter's success and happiness. This is in keeping with the tradition of Jacob who blessed his children individually, "giving each the blessing appropriate" (Genesis 49:28).

You may add these forms of blessing that were spoken of Ruth: "Blessed are you of the Lord, my daughter, for you have been kind and generous. The Lord God is your God, and his people are your people. May all the people know of certainty that you are a virtuous daughter" (Ruth 3:10; 1:16; 4:11).

A Blessing for Your Daughter

May the Lord make you like Sarah and Rebecca,
like Rachel and Leah who together built the house of Israel.
May your entire life be fruitful.
May you be favored by your husband and be blessed with children.
May the Lord's full will for you be accomplished in your life.
The Lord bless you and keep you.
The Lord cause his face to shine upon you and be gracious unto you.
The Lord turn his face toward you and give you peace.
(Speak a personal blessing expressing your wishes and
expectations for your daughter.)
Blessed are you of the Lord, my daughter,
for you have been kind and generous.

The Lord God is your God, and his people are your people.
May all the people know of certainty that you are a virtuous daughter.
May your mouth speak with wisdom.
May your heart meditate with reverence.
May your hands do the work that God has given you. May your feet
hasten to follow the path that God has laid out for your life.
May the Spirit of the Lord, the spirit of wisdom and
understanding, the spirit of counsel and power,
the spirit of knowledge and the fear of the Lord be upon you.
May the grace of our Lord Jesus Christ,
the love of God, and the fellowship of the Holy Spirit
be upon you both now and forever.
Amen.

You may also add these charges: "May your mouth speak with wisdom. May your heart meditate with reverence. May your hands do the work that God has given you. May your feet hasten to follow the path that God has laid out for your life."

You may also invoke the seven-fold Spirit of God upon your daughter: "May the Spirit of the Lord, the spirit of wisdom and understanding, the spirit of counsel and power, the spirit of knowledge and the fear of the Lord be upon you."

You may conclude with this blessing: "May the grace of our Lord Jesus Christ, the love of God, and the fellowship of the Holy Spirit be upon you both now and forever. Amen."

Blessings for Occasions

According to the Jewish tradition, there is virtually no event or circumstance in life that is not an occasion for a blessing of praise to God. Every life situation is also an opportunity for extending God's blessing to others through our prayers and benedictions.

This is in keeping with Paul's instruction: "Give thanks in all circumstances, for this is God's will for you in Christ Jesus" (1 Thessalonians 5:18). Too often Christians have little or no thought of stopping to thank God and to bless one another as the events of their lives unfold. Thankfulness and blessing should become an automatic response in the mind and heart of every believer.

If we adopt the mindset that King David had, we "will bless the LORD at all times" (Psalm 34:1). Out of our mouths will proceed blessings for God and for one another. When we begin to think in terms of blessing, we will find that it becomes the natural thing for us to do.

Most believers, however, have been robbed of this element of spiritual health. "Who am I?" they ask. "I can't bless anyone. That's the minister's job." The reality is that every believer is a priest of God, a part of the priesthood of all believers. As such, every believer has the capacity and the charge to bless others. God distributes his grace and gifts to everyone as he wills, and each divine empowerment is for blessing the community of faith.

It is time for every believer to reclaim this ancient biblical heritage of blessing and to begin to exercise it with all the vigor and confidence that comes with authority. Every occasion that unfolds holds tremendous potential for blessing, for speaking good words into the situation, into the lives of others, and unto the name of God.

In this chapter, we outline just a few of the circumstances in which you can bless with the blessing of God. You can be creative and think of many other events as well. Open your heart to the blessing impulse that is in your spirit, and you will be amazed to find that in all things you can bless the Lord. You can also touch the lives of loved ones and even total strangers as you become an instrument of God's grace and peace.

Blessings for Meals

Christians generally bless their food before they eat, offering a short prayer to God. Interestingly enough, when God commanded Israel regarding thanks at meals, he told them to bless their God for their food *after* they had eaten: "When you have eaten and are full, then you shall bless the LORD your God for the good land which he has given you" (Deuteronomy 8:10).

This passage of Scripture is the source for the oldest blessing that exists in the Hebrew and Jewish tradition. It is called the *Birkath HaMazon*, the blessing after the meal. Maybe God thought it was easier to give thanks after one was full than to do so on an empty stomach!

Much later, the sages of Israel suggested that no food (or anything else that is pleasurable) should be enjoyed without first blessing God. They created blessings to be spoken before meals to honor God for food and beverage. First, there was the blessing for the bread: "Blessed are you, O LORD our God, King of the universe, who brings forth bread from the earth." Then, there was the blessing for the fruit of the vine: "Blessed are you, O LORD our God, King of the universe, who creates the fruit of the vine."

It is virtually certain that Jesus spoke some form of both of these blessings at meals. At the Last Supper, he gave bread to his disciples and shared the cup with them only after he had "blessed." Since the *Birkath HaMazon* after-meal blessing is the oldest practiced blessing in the Bible, it is also almost certain that Jesus and his disciples spoke the words of this blessing as well.

It is the blessing after the meal that gives continuity to the evening of Sabbath blessing that the Jewish family celebrates each week. Many blessings are given before the meal (blessing children, wife, and God). After food is enjoyed, the *Birkath HaMazon* focuses the entire family's attention on God as the provider of food not only for themselves but also for the entire world.

This blessing after the meal is given in the following manner:

The father says, "Let us say grace." The rest of the family responds, "Blessed be the Name of the Lord from this time forth and for ever." The father continues, "We will bless him of whose bounty we have partaken." The family responds, "Blessed is he of whose bounty we have partaken and through whose goodness we live."

Then the family blesses God as the one who "feeds the whole world" and as the one through whom "food has never failed us." Next, as the Lord commanded, the family blesses God "for the good land which [God] has given you." These blessings are a response to God's specific command in Deuteronomy. During the second century of the common era, the Jewish people added a third petition to this blessing, asking God to "have mercy upon Israel, upon Jerusalem, upon the house of David, and upon the temple," and to ensure that they would "have need only of God's helping hand."

Christian Blessings

Jesus always blessed God and give thanks before he ate. He did so at the Last Supper. "Jesus took some bread, and after a blessing, He broke it and gave it to the disciples, and said, 'Take, eat; this is my body'" (Matthew 26:26). "Then he took the cup, and gave thanks [blessed], and gave it to them, saying, 'Drink from it, all of you' " (Matthew 26:17).

Jesus also blessed God before he miraculously fed the multitudes. "Then he commanded the multitudes to sit down on the grass. And he took the five loaves and the two fish, and looking up to heaven, he *blessed* and broke and gave the loaves to the disciples; and the disciples gave to the multitudes." (Matthew 14:19, emphasis added).

Paul also instructed believers that they should continue this biblically Hebraic tradition in blessing God (giving thanks): "Every creature of God *is* good, and nothing is to be refused if it is received with thanksgiving" (1 Timothy 4:4).

Blessings for Holidays

Holidays are not just days off from work. They are, as the word indicates, designed by God to be "Holy Days." This means that they are times set apart to give us a chance to catch our breath from the hustle and bustle of life, and remember the things that are most important in our lives: God and our families. This is especially true of those times that God has asked us to set apart on our calendars to remember the great events of salvation history.

In reality, God has made appointments on his own calendar to meet with his children, and has invited us to set aside the other demands of life and meet with him at those times. These appointments include daily hours of prayer, weekly Sabbaths, seasonal festivals, and generational celebrations. Because it is so easy for us to forget, these appointments on our spiritual calendar help us to remember. They give us opportunity to draw close to God and to our families and friends, something that all too easily gets crowded out unless we take the time to schedule it. When we follow God's appointment calendar, our whole balance of focus changes

A Blessing Before a Meal

We bless your name, O Lord our God, Sovereign of the universe,

for the bounty of the earth and for the food that you have created

and so graciously provided to strengthen and sustain our bodies.

May you bless our fellowship through the name of your Son Jesus,

our Lord, in the power of the Holy Spirit.

Amen.

A Blessing After a Meal

Blessed are you, O Lord our God, King of the universe,
who feeds the whole world with your goodness,
with grace, with loving kindness and tender mercy.
Through your great goodness, we have never lacked for food.
Blessed are you, O Lord, who gives food to all.
We thank you, O Lord our God, because you have given us a desirable,
good, and ample land. We thank you for the food wherewith you
constantly feed and sustain us every day, our daily bread.
We bless your name even as it is written:
'You shall eat and be satisfied, and you shall bless the Lord your God
for the good land which he has given you.'
Blessed are you, O Lord, for the land and for the food.

because we are constantly reminded of what is really important in life: God and our families and friends.

In a tradition of the Jewish people that was almost certainly in place during the time of Jesus and the apostles, a special form of the daily prayer that is the central prayer of Jewish life is prayed on holy days. Personal concerns are omitted so that one's entire attention on the holy days is focused on God and not on oneself.

This prayer of blessing is called the *Amidah* because it is spoken while standing. It is so important that it is also called "The Prayer." If Jesus prayed this prayer (and it is very likely that he did when he shared worship with his Jewish family in temple and synagogue), it should also have significant value for Christians as well.

A Blessing Prayer for Special Times

An Edited Form of the Festival or Sabbath Amidah (May be read responsively)

O Lord, open our lips, and our mouths shall declare your praise.

Blessed are you, O Lord our God and God of our fathers, Abraham, Isaac, and Jacob; the great, mighty and revered God, the Most High God, who bestows loving kindnesses, and is Master of all things; who remembers the pious deeds of the patriarchs, and in love will bring redemption to their children's children for your Name's sake.

O King, Helper, Savior, and Shield. Blessed are you, O Lord, the Shield of Abraham.

You, O Lord, are mighty forever; you revive the dead; you are mighty to save. You sustain the living with loving kindness, revive the dead with great mercy, support the falling, heal the sick, free the bound, and keep your faith to them that sleep in the dust. Who is like unto you, Lord of mighty acts, and who resembles you, O King, who orders death and restores life, and causes salvation to spring forth? Yes, faithful are you to revive the dead. Blessed are you, O Lord, who resurrects the dead.

We will sanctify your Name in the world even as they sanctify it in the highest heavens, as it is written by the hand of thy prophet: And they called one unto another and said,

Holy, holy, holy is the Lord of hosts: the whole earth is full of his glory.

The others say,

Blessed be the glory of the Lord from his place.

And in thy Holy Word it is written, saying

The Lord shall reign forever; your God, O Zion, unto all generations. Praise the Lord.

Unto all generations we will declare your greatness, and to all eternity we will proclaim your holiness. Your praise, O Lord our God, shall not depart from our mouth forever, for you are a great and holy God and King. Blessed are you, O Lord, the holy God.

You favor man with knowledge and teach mortals understanding.

You have favored us with knowledge of your Word and have taught us to perform your will. You have made a distinction, O Lord our God, between holy and profane, between light and darkness, between Israel and the nations, between the Sabbath and the six working days. O our Father, our

King, grant that the days which are approaching us may begin for us in peace and that we may be withheld from all sin and cleansed from all iniquity and cleave to the reverence of your name.

Blessed are you, O Lord our God, who sanctifies Israel and the festive seasons.

O Lord our God, accept your people Israel and their prayer; restore the service to the inner sanctuary of your house; receive in love and favor both the offerings of Israel and their prayer; and may the worship of your people Israel be ever acceptable unto you.

Our God and God of our fathers! May our remembrance ascend, come, and be accepted before you, with the remembrance of our fathers, of Messiah the Son of David your servant, of Jerusalem your holy city, and of all your people, the house of Israel, bringing deliverance and well-being, grace, loving kindness and mercy, life and peace on this time of celebration.

Remember us, O Lord our God, thereon for our well-being; be mindful of us for blessing, and save us unto life: by your promise of salvation and mercy, spare us, and be gracious unto us; have mercy upon us, and save us; for our eyes are bent upon you, because you are a gracious and merciful God and King. Let our eyes behold your return in mercy to Zion. Blessed are you, O Lord, who restores your divine presence unto Zion.

We give thanks unto you, for you are the Lord our God and the God of our fathers for ever and ever; you are the Rock of our lives, the Shield of our salvation through every generation.

We will give thanks unto you and declare your praise for our lives, which are committed unto your hand, and for our souls, which are in your charge, and for your miracles, which are daily with us, and for your wonders and your benefits, which are wrought at all times, evening, morn, and noon. You who are all good, whose mercies fail not, you, merciful God, whose loving kindnesses never cease, we have ever hoped in you.

Grant peace, welfare, blessing, grace, loving kindness, and mercy unto us and unto all Israel, your people. Bless us, O our Father, even all of us together, with the light of your countenance; for by the light of your countenance, you have given us, O Lord our God, the Word of life, loving kindness and righteousness, blessing, mercy, life, and peace; and may it be good in your sight to bless your people Israel at all times and in every hour with your peace.

Blessed are you, O Lord, who blesses your people Israel with peace.

O my God! guard my tongue from evil and my lips from speaking guile. Let the words of my mouth and the meditation of my heart be acceptable before you, O Lord, my Rock and my Redeemer. He who makes peace in his high places, may he make peace for us and for all Israel. Amen.

Blessings for Births

The birth of every child should be a time for joy and celebration. Children should be the fruit of love confirmed by a life-long covenant between godly parents and God. This is God's design in creating marriage: "Has not the Lord made them one? In flesh and spirit they are his. And why one? Because he was seeking godly offspring" (Malachi 2:15).

A Blessing for Your Newborn Child

Blessed are you, O Lord our God, for the bounty of your provision

in our lives. We give you praise for the gift of our child.

Thank you that you have preserved its mother's health.

As you have commanded, we bless this, your child:

The Lord bless you and keep you.

The Lord cause his face to shine upon you and be gracious unto you.

The Lord turn his face toward you and give you peace.

May the grace of our Lord Jesus Christ, the love of God our Father,

and the fellowship of the Holy Spirit be upon you,

my child, both now and forever.

Amen.

Children are not an accident of nature. They are God's gift. "Behold, children are a gift of the LORD, The fruit of the womb is a reward" (Psalm 127:3). If they are indeed God's reward to loving parents, then God should be praised and blessed when they are received. It is highly appropriate to speak words of blessing into the life of an infant child, even the words that God commanded to be spoken over the children of Israel.

When Isaac was weaned, Abraham had a great celebration (Genesis 21:8). This was an indication of the value that he placed on his son and the gratitude that he had to God for his gift to Sarah and himself.

As a Christian believer, you understand that God has entrusted you with the life of your infant child. You have been assigned as a guardian with the responsibility of nurturing and instructing your child from infancy in the ways of God. You are responsible for providing food, clothing, and shelter for your child and for maintaining a secure environment of safety and blessing.

One way in which you can keep this responsibility foremost in your life is by blessing your child regularly, even weekly as the biblical peoples did. The time to begin is at birth. (Actually, you can speak God's blessing over your child even before birth!)

Blessings for Graduations

Study and learning have always been considered sacred in the biblically Judaic tradition. The Wisdom Books of Holy Scripture extol the virtue of acquiring knowledge, understanding, and wisdom. They also exhort young men and women to study God's Word and to do it with all diligence.

There is no biblical distinction between spiritual understanding and secular knowledge. All knowledge springs from the heart of God who breathes insight into the human heart and mind (Job 32:8). In the Hebraic tradition, therefore, a father has the responsibility of teaching his children the Word of God and of equipping them with a means of livelihood. Both spiritual insight and secular understanding are essential to happy, healthy, and productive lives.

A Blessing for Your Graduate

*Pursue instruction rather than silver. Acquire knowledge
rather than fine gold. Know wisdom and understanding, justice,
judgment, and equity. Give to the young knowledge and discretion.
A wise man will hear and increase learning,
and a man of understanding will attain wise counsel.
The fear of the LORD is the beginning of knowledge.
Wisdom is the principal thing; therefore get wisdom.
And in all your getting, get understanding. Take firm hold of
instruction, do not let go; keep her, for she is your life.
Fear God, and keep his commandments:
for this is the whole duty of man.*
(Proverbs 8:10; 1:2-7; 4:7, 13)

There is also a long-standing tradition among the Jewish people in which a teacher blesses his students. This parallels the blessing that parents give their children. It also underscores the importance that education and educators have in the lives of growing and maturing children. Parents are the first teachers. Then, others become stewards of the process of learning, adding knowledge, understanding, and wisdom.

Graduations are important milestones that mark educational accomplishment. They are rites of passage from one level of knowledge and understanding to another and finally into a position where all that has been acquired can be put to work to provide stable, secure, and joyful lives, families, and communities.

Blessings for Rites of Passage

In ancient times and in many cultures, the time at which children reached puberty was considered an important event. Various rites of passage were used to mark this time of transition from childhood to adolescence.

In the Jewish culture, a long-standing practice has recognized this stage of development. For boys, it is called *Bar Mitzvah* (Son of the Commandment); for girls, it is called *Bat Mitzvah* (Daughter of the Commandment). For boys, it is the age of thirteen; for girls it is the age of twelve. Originally, the achievement of this status required no ceremony; however, in more modern times, ceremony and blessing have become common.

This is the time that the child takes on full responsibility for his or her own actions. The child normally says, "Today I am a man (or woman)." The child is invited to make *aliyah* by "going up" to recite the customary blessing over the weekly Scripture reading. This is also a time for public demonstration of the child's understanding of his or her faith and of the Torah, the Word of God.

This practice is likely the source of some Christian understanding that children reach an "age of accountability," when they alone become responsible before God and society for their actions. There is no specific scriptural definition of the age at which this occurs; however, its connection with the onset of adolescence is certainly appropriate.

A Blessing when Adolescence Begins

Blessed are you, O Lord our God, Sovereign of the universe,
who has brought us to this day by your mercy.
We thank you for this wonderful life that you have entrusted
to our care. Now, we return him (her) to you
and charge him (her) to be upright before you.
_____, we will ever be thankful to God
for giving you to us as an inheritance from his grace.
Now, as you come to this transition in life,
we surrender you into his hands alone.
You are now responsible and accountable before God
for your actions. We promise to love and support you
in the coming years as your grow into adulthood.

We bless you with the blessing that God commanded for his children:
The Lord bless you and keep you. The Lord cause his face
to shine upon you and be gracious unto you.
The Lord turn his face toward you and give you peace.
May the Spirit of the Lord, the spirit of wisdom and understanding,
the spirit of counsel and power, the spirit of knowledge and
the fear of the Lord be upon you.
May your mouth speak with wisdom. May your heart
meditate with reverence. May your hands do the work
that God has given you. May your feet hasten to follow
the path that God has laid out for your life.
May the grace of our Lord Jesus Christ, the love of God,
and the fellowship of the Holy Spirit be upon you
both now and forever.
Amen.

In many Christian communions, a similar experience is celebrated in Confirmation. This practice gives recognition of the child's accomplishment in understanding and commitment to Christian faith. Many fellowships, however, let this important time in a child's development pass with hardly any notice.

In a time when dramatic hormonal and physical changes are taking place in a child's life, is it not even more important that strong affirmation and commitment to God and his Word be manifest and that continuing parental support is affirmed for the decision-making process that the adolescent must begin to assume? A public or private family celebration of this time is certainly in order with appropriate blessings.

Blessings for Weddings

Weddings are among the most important events in life. Marriage was instituted by God in the beginning so that one man and one woman might be joined for life in a covenant with God, bound in loving commitment to one another and to the family that they become. God has made two one so that godly children might be brought into a secure and stable environment of love and support (Malachi 2:15). He has brought two parts of a whole together so that both together may be complete, balancing and complementing each the other.

Traditional approaches to weddings have begun with the father of the bride "giving" his daughter to be married to the groom. This practice, however, has come to be seen as a perpetuation of the medieval belief that women were chattel, virtually owned by either father or husband.

A modern device has come to be added to the wedding ceremony in which the parents of both bride and groom offer their blessing upon the couple. This may be a simple response of "we do" to the minister's question, "Who blesses this marriage." It may also be more involved with one or all parents speaking personal blessings into the lives of their children. Whatever the case, this should be done tastefully in a supportive manner. Options are as many and varied as the creativity of bride and groom and their parents.

A Parent's Wedding Blessing
for the Bride

What a rare find is a capable wife! She is worth far more than rubies.

May your husband put his full confidence in you

and never lack anything of value. May you bring him good,

not harm, all the days of your life.

May you always be strong and your health be vigorous so that

you may watch over the affairs of your home.

May your arms always be extended to the poor and the needy.

May you be clothed with strength and dignity.

May God give you wisdom, and may faithful instruction

be always on your tongue.

Many women have done well, but you will surpass them all.
You have been a treasure to us, a gift and a heritage
from the Lord. We are thankful that God has entrusted us
with your life and has allowed us to nurture you unto this time.
As you now join with your beloved to create a new home,
we bless you with all the blessings of heaven and earth.
May the Lord answer you when you are in distress.
May he remember your sacrifices and give you the desires
of your heart. May you enjoy the fruit of your labor and
may prosperity and blessing be yours.
May the Lord bless you all the days of your life, and
may you live to bless and enjoy your children's children.

A Parent's Wedding Blessing for the Groom

Blessed is the man who fears the LORD, who delights greatly

in his commandments. The generations that follow you

will be blessed because of your righteousness.

May you be gracious to your wife and full of compassion,

and righteous. May you never be afraid.

Let your heart always be steadfast, trusting in the LORD.

May you always remember to give to the poor

and conduct your affairs generously and with justice

so that wealth and riches may be in your own house.

You have been a treasure to us,
a gift and a heritage from the Lord.
We are thankful that God has entrusted us with your life and has
allowed us to nurture you unto this time.
As you now join with your beloved to create a new home,
we bless you with all the blessings of heaven and earth.
May the Lord answer you when you are in distress.
May he remember your sacrifices and give you the desires
of your heart. May you enjoy the fruit of your labor and
may prosperity and blessing be yours.
May the Lord bless you all the days of your life,
and may you live to bless and enjoy
your children's children.

The important part of this exercise is the solidarity of parental support for the creation of a new family and the giving of parental blessings in the tradition of the ancient Hebrews.

Blessings for the Bereaved

In our human situation, we always look on the finality of death with sorrow. We are suddenly and often without warning separated by death from a loved one. We grieve at our loss. Try our best, we cannot escape the fact that it is appointed unto men to die. The one thing that is certain about life is that it is terminal.

Death is the great equalizer. It comes to all men, rich and poor, powerful and helpless. At a time of bereavement, the Jewish people follow the example of Job who sat on the ground and was silent before the Lord. At the same time, however, they recognize that God is to be blessed in all things, even in the pain and sorrow of death.

In the biblically Hebraic tradition blessing is not something that is reserved only for the good things that happen in life. It is equally appropriate in reaction to those things that are or seem to be bad. This is true of death and bereavement as well as of life. As a matter of fact, the Scriptures suggest that the day of death is better than that of birth (Ecclesiastes 7:1).

When David declared, "I will bless the Lord at all times; his praise shall continually be in my mouth" (Psalm 34:1), he did not exclude the sorrow that life brings. He understood that God is sovereign over all and, like Paul, he believed that "all things work together for good to them that love God" (Romans 8:28).

Job understood this biblical principle and may well have set the example for the tradition that follows to this day among the Jewish people: "The Lord has given, and the Lord has taken away. Blessed be the name of the Lord" (Job 1:20). Job had just experienced the savage attack of Satan against his family and his fortune. All was lost. He was alone and afflicted with boils from head to toe. Could anything have been worse?

Job had the wisdom to recognize that God was the source of everything that he had possessed, and he had the courage to praise and bless the Lord even in the disaster that had befallen him. He trusted that God was in control and that everything would take place according to God's purposes for his life.

Job also knew that even death was not final. "I know that my Redeemer lives, and that in the end he will stand upon the earth. And after my skin has been destroyed, yet in my flesh I will see God; I myself will see him with my own eyes—I, and not another" (Job 19:25-27). Job believed in the resurrection at the last day: "For there is hope for a tree, if it is cut down, that it will sprout again, and that its tender shoots will not cease. Though its root may grow old in the earth, and its stump may die in the ground, yet at the scent of water it will bud and bring forth branches like a plant ... Oh, that you would hide me in the grave, that you would conceal me until your wrath is past, that you would appoint me a set time, and remember me! If a man dies, shall he live again? All the days of my hard service I will wait, till my change comes. You shall call, and I will answer you" (Job 14:7-9, 13-15).

Paul understood that death had been conquered forever by the resurrection of Jesus: "Death is swallowed up in victory ... O Death, where is your sting? ... Thanks be to God, who gives us the victory through our Lord Jesus Christ" (1 Corinthians 15:54-55, 57). "For if we believe that Jesus died and rose again, even so God will bring with Him those who sleep in Jesus ... For the Lord himself will descend from heaven with a shout, with the voice of an archangel, and with the trumpet of God. And the dead in Christ will rise first. Then we who are alive and remain shall be caught up together with them in the clouds to meet the Lord in the air. And thus we shall always be with the Lord. Therefore comfort one another with these words" (1 Thessalonians 4:14-18).

The Epistle to the Hebrews tells us: "Now may the God of peace who brought up our Lord Jesus from the dead, that great Shepherd of the sheep, through the blood of the everlasting covenant, make you complete in every good work to do His will, working in you what is well pleasing in His sight,

A Blessing for the Bereaved

The Lord gives, and the Lord has taken away:
Blessed be the name of the Lord. I know whom I have believed
and am persuaded that he is able to keep what I have
committed unto him until the day of his coming.
For the Lord himself will descend from heaven with a shout,
with the voice of an archangel, and with the trumpet of God,
and the dead in Christ will rise. I know that my Redeemer lives
and that in the end, he will stand upon the earth and
in my flesh I shall see him. O death, where is your sting?
O grave, where is your victory? Blessed be the name of the Lord
who gives us the victory through our Lord Jesus Christ.
Amen.

through Jesus Christ, to whom be glory forever and ever. Amen" (Hebrews 13:20-21).

For those who believe in the God of creation, death is merely a step into everlasting life. God is the God of the living, and he will give everlasting life to all who believe and receive the blessing of his priceless gift, his only begotten Son. If we believe this truth, we can bless the Lord in all things and trust him for life to come in the resurrection.

Blessings When Parting Company

As Shakespeare said, "Parting is such sweet sorrow!" When we must separate from loved ones and friends, we do so reluctantly, for we value and cherish the company of those who are dear to us. Our sorrow is lessened, however, by the expectation that we shall meet again, hopefully in the near future.

Since there is a blessing for virtually everything in the Bible, there should be a blessing for parting company as well. And so there is. It is found in the words of blessing and petition that Jacob offered when he and his family were leaving the company of Laban. "May the LORD keep watch between you and me when we are away from each other"(Genesis 31:49). These words were all the more powerful and poetic when Jacob named the place where they were standing "*Mitzpah*," which in Hebrew means "watchtower." It was as though the patriarch was asking God to stand as a watchtower guarding both departing families until such a time as they would come together again. Only the all-seeing eye of the Shepherd of Israel could look in both directions to guard both parties at the same time.

The Hebrew word *mitzpah* can also indicate the punishing of a trespasser. God is the one who watches over his children and keeps them from the trespasser, from the devices of *Satan*, the trap setter. When someone or something attempts to interfere, breaking the fellowship of those who trust in the Lord, he delivers them from the evil and establishes their goings.

Until this day, parting Jewish families and individuals often speak simply one word in Hebrew, "*Mitzpah*," "watchtower," understanding that God is

A Parting Blessing

I know whom I have believed and am convinced

that he is able to guard what I have entrusted unto him.

I pray that you may prosper in all things and be in health,

even as your soul prospers.

The name of the Lord is a strong tower.

We run to him, and we are safe.

May the Lord keep watch between you and me

when we are away from each other.

Mitzpah!

the one who "watches between you and me when were are away from each other." In exchange of mail or e-mail, they may also use the one-word blessing, *"Mitzpah."*

The believer who knows whom he has believed is convinced that God is able to keep all that he has committed unto him for that day (2 Timothy 1:12). "The name of the LORD is a strong tower. The righteous run to it, and they are safe" (Proverbs 18:10).

Blessings for Everyone

In the tradition of the Holy Scriptures, believers can offer God's blessings and their prayers for everyone. Indeed, the command of God is that we pray for everyone everywhere: "Therefore I exhort first of all that supplications, prayers, intercessions, and giving of thanks be made for all men ... For this is good and acceptable in the sight of God our Savior, who desires all men to be saved and to come to the knowledge of the truth" (1 Timothy 2:1, 3-4). Jesus pronounces a blessing upon those who rejoice when they are persecuted (Matthew 5:10-12)! He even exhorts Christians to bless and pray for their enemies (Luke 6:28)!

Christians should find themselves always in an attitude of blessing. James even wondered how it is possible for blessings and curses to come from the same fountain (James 3:9-10). Believers, therefore, should keep their hearts clean and their lips pure by learning to speak blessings to all in all situations. If every Christian stopped in every situation to speak or pray a blessing, the world would change overnight.

Blessings for Leaders

As Christians, there are two kinds of leaders who impact our lives: spiritual leaders and civic leaders. As a part of the divine system of oversight and protection for humankind, leaders have been appointed by God for our own welfare and blessing. Throughout the Holy Scriptures, we are instructed to give proper respect to both kinds of leaders. This includes the responsibility to pray for our leaders and to bless them in the name of the Lord.

Spiritual Leaders

Believers are admonished in the Epistle to the Hebrews: "Remember your leaders, who spoke the word of God to you. Consider the outcome of their way of life and imitate their faith ... Obey your leaders and submit to their authority. They keep watch over you as men who must give an account" (Hebrews 13:7, 17).

God spoke these words to Moses concerning the spiritual leaders of Israel: "I myself have selected your fellow Levites from among the Israelites as a gift to you, dedicated to the LORD" (Numbers 18:6). Spiritual leaders are, therefore, a gift of God's blessing to his people. It is only proper, then, that God's people should also bless their leaders, and as Aaron and Hur did for Moses, hold up their hands before the Lord, sharing the burden of leadership.

Civil Leaders

Paul has specifically instructed the church in this regard about leaders in civil government: "Everyone must submit himself to the governing authorities, for there is no authority except that which God has established. ... He is God's servant to do you good ... Therefore, it is necessary to submit to the authorities, not only because of possible punishment, but also because of conscience. This is why you pay taxes, for the authorities are God's servants, who give their full time to governing" (Romans 13:1, 3-6).

Peter added this confirmation: "Submit yourselves for the Lord's sake to every authority instituted among men: whether to the king, as the supreme authority, or to governors, who are sent by him to punish those who do wrong and to commend those who do right" (1 Peter 2:13-15).

Daniel established this divine principle: God "changes times and seasons; he sets up kings and deposes them" (Daniel 2:21). Every power that exists is governed by God. He exalts and he removes leaders as it pleases him. It is for this reason that Paul admonished believers to pray for civil authorities: "I exhort first of all that supplications, prayers, intercessions, and giving of thanks be made for all men, for kings and all who are in authority, that we may lead a quiet and peaceable life in all godliness and reverence" (1 Timothy 2:1-2).

Solomon expressed a great word of wisdom when he commanded: "Do not curse the king, even in your thought" (Ecclesiastes 10:20). Daniel repeatedly expressed the same prayer of blessing both for the kings that had brought Israel (and himself) captive and the king that liberated Israel. He exclaimed to Nebuchadnezzar, Belshazzar, and Darius: "O king, live forever" (Daniel 3:9; 5:10; 6:6). If curses are inappropriate against civil leaders and if prayers should be offered for them, then surely blessings can be spoken over them and on their behalf.

Of course, many who live in some degree of oppression may want to say the blessing that the aged rabbi suggested for the Tzar in *Fiddler on the Roof*. Since there is a blessing for virtually everything in the Jewish community, he was asked, "Is there a blessing for the Tzar?" He replied tongue, in cheek, "May the Lord bless and keep the Tzar far... away from us." Some things that God asks cannot be fully comprehended by the human understanding. We must, therefore, do what God said, expecting him to fulfill what we cannot understand.

A Blessing for Spiritual Leaders

We thank you, All-Sufficient Father, for the provision
that you have made for our protection and well being.
You have given as gifts the leaders who watch for our souls and
stand alongside us as guardians against the powers of the evil one.
We bless _____, whom you have appointed
to lead this community of faith.
May you ever guard and keep them in perfect peace
and may you strengthen them in the most holy faith.
Empower them to speak the truth in love.
Like our Lord Jesus Christ, may they keep all whom
you have committed into their care until the age to come.

A Blessing for Civil Leaders

We honor you, O God, for your infinite wisdom
in providing leaders whom you have established
to protect the innocent and to punish the wicked.
We know that you establish authorities,
setting the times of their administration.
We bless _____, whom you have
appointed to lead our society and our community.
May you give them wisdom in their tasks.
May they trust in you and uphold your law
so that the people of this community may
live their lives in peace and security, in godliness and honesty.

Blessings for Friends

There are many blessings that can be pronounced upon friends and fellow members of the community of faith.

First, you may want to adopt the practice of blessing as a form of greeting. This is what King Saul did when the Prophet Samuel came to visit him: Saul "went to meet him and to bless him." Your greeting may be a simple: "May God bless you," or it may take the form of the blessing that David said belonged to all of God's children: "The blessing of the Lord be upon you. We bless you in the name of the Lord" (Psalm 129:8).

You may wish to speak "The Blessing" into your friend or colleague's life by stretching forth your hand and saying, "The LORD bless you and keep you. The LORD cause his face to shine upon you and be gracious unto you. The LORD turn his face toward you and give you peace" (Numbers 6:24–26).

You may wish to invoke the seven-fold Spirit of God upon your friend by saying, "May the Spirit of the Lord rest upon you, the spirit of wisdom and understanding, the spirit of counsel and power, the spirit of knowledge and of the fear of the Lord" (Isaiah 11:2).

You may also use any of the New Testament blessings, including these:

"May you prosper in all things and be in health, just as your soul prospers" (3 John 1:2).

"May your whole spirit, soul, and body be preserved blameless at the coming of our Lord Jesus Christ" (1 Thessalonians 5:23).

"May the God of hope fill you with all joy and peace in believing, that you may abound in hope by the power of the Holy Spirit" (Romans 15:13).

"May the God of peace who brought up our Lord Jesus from the dead, that great Shepherd of the sheep, through the blood of the everlasting covenant, make you complete in every good work to do His will, working in you what is well pleasing in His sight, through Jesus Christ, to whom be glory forever and ever. Amen" (Hebrews 13:20-21).

"May the grace of our Lord Jesus Christ, the love of God, and the fellowship of the Holy Spirit be with you for ever" (2 Corinthians 13:14).

You may also want to make a personal blessing upon your friend. The words that come from your heart are powerful and uplifting.

Whatever the case, look your friend in the eye, make a meaningful and respectful touch with your hand, and speak your heart and the words of inspiration that God gives you for them. They will be blessed, and you will be blessed, too.

Blessings for Strangers

"Therefore love the stranger, for you were strangers in the land of Egypt" (Deuteronomy 10:19).

"The Lord protects the strangers; He supports the fatherless and the widow" (Psalm 146:9).

A Blessing for Strangers

God of Abraham, Isaac, and Jacob, we extend your blessing

beyond the reaches of our community of faith

unto all the strangers around the world.

May you protect and bless them by your grace,

and may you give them a place in your house

better than that of sons and daughters.

May you bring grace and blessing upon us all

through the tender mercies of your Son, Jesus Christ.

Amen.

"And sons of the stranger, who are joined to the LORD, to serve him, and to love the name of the LORD, to be to him for servants, every keeper of the Sabbath from polluting it, and those keeping hold on my covenant … I have given to them in my house, and within my walls a station and a name better than sons and than daughters" (Isaiah 56:6, 5).

Blessings for Enemies

"Love your enemies, bless those who curse you, do good to those who hate you, and pray for those who spitefully use you and persecute you" (Matthew 5:44).

"When we are cursed, we bless; being persecuted, we suffer it; when we are slandered, we answer kindly" (1 Corinthians 4:12-13).

"You prepare a table before me in the presence of my enemies" (Psalm 23:5).

A BLESSING FOR ENEMIES

Almighty Father, we bless those who have cursed us.

Create a table of peace before us where we can come

and be reconciled to one another and to you.

Empower us to do good unto those who have harmed us.

We pray for them and for their spiritual welfare.

May you have mercy upon us all through your Son,

our Lord, Jesus Christ.

A Blessing for the World

God of heaven and earth, we bless your name for all of your creation.
The earth is the Lord's and the fullness thereof,
the world and they who dwell herein.
We extend your blessing in petition for all men everywhere
through our supplications, prayers, and intercessions,
and we give you thanks that you have created all humanity
in your image and likeness and for the purpose of glorifying
your name in the earth. We pray that the blessing of salvation
through Jesus Christ our Lord will come unto all people everywhere
so that the knowledge of the glory of the Lord
will cover the earth as the waters cover the sea.
May the God of peace bring the blessing of peace to all the earth,
through the name of the Prince of Peace,
Jesus Christ, the Lord. Amen.

Blessings for the World

"Therefore I exhort first of all that supplications, prayers, intercessions, and giving of thanks be made for all men ... for this *is* good and acceptable in the sight of God our Savior, who desires all men to be saved and to come to the knowledge of the truth" (1 Timothy 2:1, 3-4).

"For God so loved the world that He gave His only begotten Son, that whoever believes in Him should not perish but have everlasting life" (John 3:16).

Blessings of Petition

When God entered into covenant with Abraham, he swore that he would fulfill the covenant throughout all generations. Abraham knew that the blessing was secure from the first moment that God spoke it; however, he frequently approached God for reconfirmation of that blessing. As he and his wife aged, he turned to God for reassurance that their expectations for an heir would be fulfilled. God did not rebuke him for "unbelief." Instead, he embraced him in his grace and reiterated the covenant and the promise.

Later Jacob wrestled with his own fears that the promise that had been given to his grandfather would fail in his generation. At one point, Jacob even wrestled with the Lord. He contended for the blessing, saying, "I will not let you go until you bless me" (Genesis 32:26). His insistence on having the blessing brought him a new identity. He was thereafter called "Israel," God's prince. God was ever present to reassure Jacob of his support in each situation of life that he encountered. The covenant and the blessing were reiterated, reestablished, and reconfirmed

This is a clear example of the interconnection between blessing and petition. God will never reject one who engages him with such passion and intensity. Believers today, like Jacob of old, often need a reconfirmation of God's promise and blessing. This is not a manifestation of unbelief. It is simply a human need to be reassured in the face of a new encounter or a new challenge.

It is proper for individuals to approach the Heavenly Father as his children, seeking his favor and his blessing. A prominent example is recorded in the Psalms where David offered this form of the Aaronic benediction as a petition for blessing: "God be merciful unto us, and bless us, and cause his face to shine upon us" (Psalm 67:1). This was a petition, a prayer invoking the divine presence to bless by turning his face toward his people. The wording is virtually quoted from "The Blessing."

Another example of petitionary blessing is found in the prayer blessing of Jabez. Though he was a rather obscure character in Scripture, Jabez boldly offered these words of petition: "O that you would bless me indeed and enlarge my border, and that your hand might be with me, and that you would keep me from harm that it may not pain me!" (1 Chronicles 4:10).

In this case, Jabez requested a personal blessing for himself, expressing his hope that God bring both physical and spiritual benefits to him. First, he hoped that God would expand the range of his resources. Then he prayed that God would keep him from suffering. Is this not the very center of petition in the Lord's Prayer: "Give us this day our daily bread . . . and deliver us from evil" (Matthew 6:13)? Would God even consider a such a petition of self-blessing and grant it? The answer is found in Scripture itself: "God granted [Jabez] what he requested."

Jesus himself underscored the nature of prayer in the illustration of the widow and the unjust judge, noting that the judge granted the widow's petition because she inconvenienced him. The Master concluded that if such an unjust jurist would answer the unrelenting petition of his subject, how much more would the Just Judge grant the prayers of his children (Luke 18:6-7). This is why the writer of Hebrews urges all believers to "come boldly unto the throne of grace, that we may obtain mercy, and find grace to help in time of need" (Hebrews 4:16). The word *boldly* means "frankly, with fearless confidence." There is, therefore, no hint of timidity or reserve that should be exercised when approaching "the throne of grace," the seat of divine authority, to petition God for the blessing of his grace and mercy. One can have both humility and boldness when he petitions the Almighty.

Jesus also made it clear that if a child of the kingdom asks the Heavenly Father for bread, he will not be given a stone (Matthew 7:9). If he asks for fish, he will not be given a serpent. Anyone who comes to God must believe that God exists and that he is a rewarder of those who diligently seek him (Hebrews 11:6). One knows this for certain because Jesus Christ is the same yesterday, today, and forever (Hebrews 13:8). The believer has an advocate with the Father who is touched with his deepest need (1 John 2:1; Hebrews 4:15). Jesus will never drive away anyone who comes to him

A Blessing of Petition for
Divine Protection, Provision, and Personal Concerns

Almighty God, be merciful unto us and bless us,
and cause your face to shine upon us. We come boldly
unto your throne of grace, that we may obtain mercy and find grace
to help in our time of need. Bless us indeed, let your might be with us,
and keep us from harm. Give us today our daily bread.
We will never cease to seek your face until you bless us
in your tender mercies. We are the children of your covenant
through Jesus Christ our Lord; therefore, we believe that
you will give us the desires of our heart as they accomplish your will.
Accept our petition of praise as we exalt your name, Most High God.
Amen.

in faith (John 6:37). He is always filled with compassion, and he stretches forth his hand of blessing to those who approach him in faith.

The boldness to petition God for blessing is well within our entitlements as believers; however, we often have not because we ask not or because we ask amiss (James 4:2-3). God will welcome his children with open arms, place his hand upon them, and speak his everlasting benediction into their lives. When we contend for the blessing, we can be certain that he will give it to us in inconceivable dimensions. We already have his assurance that we need only ask and we will receive (Luke 11:9). It's really that simple!

Releasing God to Bless

How can we be certain that God will bless us in every way that is according to his will? Are there obstacles that hinder us from being blessed? Can we discover the biblical secret of releasing God to bless everything that we put our hand to do? As with many questions of this nature, the answer is so simple that it is too simple.

Treasure and Tithe

God is man's source. God's will is that all men should be blessed beyond all measure of their own expectations. In order for God to bless, however, we must recognize that we are completely dependent upon his provision for our sustenance. We prove that God is our source by returning to him what he asks of us in tithes and offerings.

God has designed it so that when we give him the tenth (tithe) of our gain, it is as though we have given him everything. The Hebrew word for tithe, *mesher*, means both "a tenth" and "a very large amount, abundance, or wealth." When we give the tenth, we demonstrate to God that we are giving all. We do not seek to hold on to what we have gained as though we had acquired it through our own strength. We return to God what he requires because we know he has given us everything that we possess.

The act of tithing is, therefore, the mechanism that releases God to bless us. God specifically confirms this in his Word: "Bring the whole tithe to my storehouse ... Test me in this ... and see if I will not open the floodgates of heaven and pour out so much blessing that you will not have room enough for it" (Malachi 3:10). God promises that if we fully tithe into his treasury, the floodgates of heaven will open with an amazing array of blessings.

Most Christians have been confronted with the issue of tithes from and entirely negative standpoint. They have been warned by church authorities of the curses that will come upon them if they fail to tithe.

Church bureaucracies have insisted that their treasuries are "God's storehouse" and that all of the tithe must come into their local congregation or into their denomination. This negative approach has made tithing seem like a burden and a curse instead of a blessing. As a result, many Christians either do not tithe at all or they do so with the same cheerfulness they give to paying taxes!

The tithe is designed by God to provide a divine vehicle for blessing. "Give, and you shall receive," Jesus said (Luke 6:38). The first blessing is to the one who gives: the tither. By obeying God's command, we release God to bless. The second blessing is to those who receive the tithe. This may be our local congregations or it may be ministries that are enriching our lives and the lives of others. It may also be our giving to the underprivileged of society.

God's Blessing System

The tenth of increase was considered holy or separated unto the Lord (Leviticus 27:30). Israel was commanded to bring the firstfruits of its harvests (the tithe) to the Lord. When one had fully tithed and confessed his heritage, he was to attest that he had taken the tithes out of his house and had brought them to the priesthood, thereby fulfilling God's commandment.

Once he had made this affirmation, he was permitted to pray this petition for blessing: "Look down from heaven, your holy dwelling place, and bless your people Israel and the land you have given us" (Deuteronomy 26:15). The declaration of blessing was then placed upon the worshipper: "You have declared this day that the LORD is your God and you will walk in his ways ... The LORD has declared this day that you are his people, his treasured possession" (Deuteronomy 26:17-18).

Because the believer had brought his treasure to God, he was declared God's treasure! Then God promised, "And all these blessings shall come upon you and overtake you, because you obey the voice of the LORD your God: The LORD will command the blessing on you ... in all to which you set your hand. The LORD will open the heavens, the storehouse of his bounty" (Deuteronomy 28:8; 28:12).

The language here is exactly what Malachi promises: the windows of heaven will be open with uncontainable blessing to those who demonstrate their dependence and faithfulness to God through the act of tithing.

Such obedience is foundational to receiving God's blessing, for God can never bless that which he does not approve. King David succinctly described this divine law: "Delight yourself in the Lord, and he will give you the desires of your heart. Commit your way to the Lord, trust also in him, and he will do it" (Psalm 37:3-4).

The blessings of God are secure unto those who fulfill the instructions of his Word. Listen to this promise: "Now it shall be, if you diligently obey the Lord your God, being careful to do all his commandments … all these blessings will come upon you and overtake you if you obey the Lord your God" (Deuteronomy 28:1-2). The blessings of God are inescapable for those who love God and demonstrate their love as Abraham did through faithfulness to God's will and Word.

Tithing and giving, then, are the scriptural means of preparing a highway for a convoy of God's blessings. Those who are obedient to God's commandments in regard to money and other resources discover that they release God to bless all the works of their hands. Their generosity causes their entire human experience to be filled with the divine light. It is the key to the strongbox of God's treasure, and it is divine insurance that the richest of God's blessings will always belong to them.

The One-Word Blessing

Is it possible to encapsulate all of God's blessing for man in one word? Can everything that God has for people be summed up in one word? If the apostle understood that all that God is can be expressed in the word *love* (1 John 4:8), why would it not also be possible to focus God's desires for us in one word?

From the record of Scripture, it would appear so. One biblical word has continually echoed God's blessing for us across the corridors of time. It is the Hebrew word *shalom*, which fundamentally means "peace," but also means much more than that. It means peace in the sense of the absence of conflict. It means health and security. It means completeness, soundness, tranquility, and contentment. It means quietness and prosperity. In short, it means everything that human beings need.

Shalom

Shalom is the final word in "The Blessing" that God dictated to Moses to be placed upon his children throughout their generations. *Shalom* has always been and will always be God's final word for humankind. The blessing of the Lord brings peace, as David declared: "The Lord will bless his people with peace [*shalom*]" (Psalm 29:11).

Perhaps for this reason, the word *shalom* has become both the greeting and the goodbye for the Jewish people for generations. One does not say, "Hello," or "Goodbye" in Israel. One simply says, *"Shalom!"* Could it be that the overriding concern among the Hebrew people for expressing blessing in every life situation came to be vocalized in this one word: "*Shalom*," the final word of God's blessing?

David recognized that the future of a man of integrity is *shalom* (Psalm 37:37). Solomon understood that God's commandments brought long life and *shalom* (Proverbs 3:2). Isaiah believed that God would keep the person who trusted in the Lord in perfect *shalom* (Isaiah 26:3). Jeremiah foresaw that after much trouble, God would restore *shalom* to his people (Jeremiah 33:6). Even the pagan kings Nebuchadnezzar and Darius addressed their subjects by saying, "*Shalom* be unto you" (Daniel 4:1; 6:25). Haggai's prophetic promise was, "In this place I will give *shalom* " (Haggai 2:9).

Isaiah predicted that a child would be born in Israel who would bear the title, "Prince of Peace," the "*Sar Shalom*" (Isaiah 9:6). He continued by declaring that of the increase of his *shalom* there would be no end (Isaiah 9:7). When the child that the prophet predicted was born, angels made this proclamation to Judean shepherds: "Glory to God in the highest, and on earth *shalom* to men on whom his favor rests" (Luke 2:14, NIV). As he walked among men, the Prince of Peace continually spoke this blessing:

"Shalom!" He said it when he calmed the raging sea (Mark 4:39). He repeated it when he healed the sick (Luke 8:48). He spoke the calming word twice to his troubled disciples when he appeared to them after the resurrection (John 20:19, 21). "Grace and peace be unto you" became Paul's familiar greeting in his letters to the churches (Romans 1:7; 1 Corinthians 1:3; Galatians 1:3; Ephesians 1:2). Peter, John, and Jude also used the same greeting.

There is, then, a one-word blessing that speaks all of God's intentions for mankind. It is the word *shalom.* And there is a peace that passes all understanding (Philippians 4:7), the *shalom* of God that he has promised and will ever give to his children. In the time when the Messiah shall come, he will bring universal peace. The entire world then will hear the final word of God's blessing for man: *Shalom!*

O that all people everywhere would join in a mighty, resounding chorus that would echo unto the ends of the earth, speaking in unison God's one-word blessing: *"Shalom!"* Yes, may there be peace on earth speedily and in our lifetime!

God's Final Blessing

It is safe to say that in everything God will have the last word. The first thing that God did in creation was to bless humankind, and the last thing that he will do with when his kingdom finally comes is to bless them. In Eden, God blessed Adam and Eve by giving them dominion over all the earth. In the end, God will bless all the righteous with these words: "Come, you blessed of my Father, inherit the kingdom prepared for you from the beginning of the world" (Matthew 25:34). God's original blessing will be God's final blessing.

God is ever a blessing God. With God, there was blessing in the beginning, there will be blessing in the end, and there is blessing everywhere in between. His mercies never end. They are new every morning. Great is his faithfulness (Lamentations 3:22-23).

Therefore, with David, we will "sing of the mercies of the LORD forever," making known his faithfulness to all generations (Psalm 89:1). With Paul we exclaim, "Blessed be the God and Father of our Lord Jesus Christ, who has blessed us with every spiritual blessing in heavenly places in Christ" (Ephesians 1:3). And with John and the holy angels and the millions of saints, we proclaim: "Blessing, and honor, and glory, and power, be to him that sits on the throne, and to the Lamb for ever and ever" (Revelation 5:13).

Epilogue

Restoration and Blessing

A Personal Word

One of the amazing things that God has been doing in our time is the work of restoring the Hebraic foundations of the Christian faith. This is truly a work of the Holy Spirit. People of every denomination and ethnic group from around the world are now intently searching for and finding long-lost secrets about the biblical origins of Christianity.

Understanding the Hebraic roots of our faith is a golden key that continually unlocks the treasures of Holy Scripture. These truths give us assurance that God's covenant faithfulness is a rock of stability in which we can trust. The faith of Jesus and the apostles becomes clear and simple and easy to incorporate into our lives when we understand it in its original biblical context.

No greater example of God's unchanging hand could be offered than in the subject of divine blessing. God determined to bless humanity in the beginning, and nothing has ever stopped him from finishing his quest. Our Heavenly Father has literally moved all of heaven and earth to ensure that his original blessing for the human race would be fulfilled in his final blessing.

The subject of blessing is just a single drop of water in an ocean of understanding that awaits those who are passionate about searching the Scriptures. There is so much more to be studied, so much more to be learned. We have only begun to see a glimmer of a light that is too wonderful to imagine, a light that will soon brighten our pathway.

We are, in effect, sifting through the rubble of men's ideas that have covered over the bedrock of truth and the foundation stones of our faith. We are working our way through layer after layer of ideas that have been piled on top of the original faith that was once delivered to the saints. But we are making wonderful discoveries of long-obscured truth.

For over forty years I have been researching and writing, teaching and preaching foundational truths about original Christianity. One of the greatest blessings of my life has been the inspiration to study, to learn, to do, and to teach these important concepts and to see the lives of believers changed dramatically when they, too, see the truth.

For many years, I have led the ministry of Restoration Foundation, a transdenominational networking organization specializing in Christian education and publishing. We have focused on connecting people with people and people with information about the Jewish roots of our Christian faith.

Restoration Foundation has become a rock-solid source for theologically sound and historically accurate teaching that is presented in a non-threatening, non-judgmental way. We have learned that if we simply share the insights that God has given us and allow the Holy Spirit to lead and guide believers into truth, the results are a wonderful blessing for all.

We are privileged to edit and publish *Restore!*, a cutting-edge journal that brings sound scholarship to bear on issues of vital importance to the church at large. Through this vehicle, we have been able to enrich the lives of countless people with restoration truths and practices. Our network of dedicated Christians has helped believers around the world recover the roots of their faith without fear of legalism or distortion.

We also have produced many of the leading books that offer scholarly and inspirational teaching on various aspects of our biblical heritage. Other teaching materials also make it possible for Christians to understand their Hebrew Lord and his will for their lives with greater clarity. We consider it a privilege to serve the body of Christ in this new rediscovery of our ancient faith traditions.

Jesus well said it: "You shall know the truth, and the truth shall make you free." The glorious liberty that truth brings is exhilarating, but it is also awesome as well. The challenge of Hebraic faith is to study so that we may do what God has said. When we become doers of the Word of God, we actually find ourselves teaching others through our example.

I trust that as you have read this volume you have discovered new biblical truth and the blessing that it brings to those who discover it and make it a part of their lives. You will now find yourself increasingly hungry to learn more about the Jewish roots of your faith. Let me assure you that there is a treasure house of understanding awaiting you as you use your own golden key to open the floodgates of God's blessings.

May we together commit ourselves to the task of finding our way back home: back to the Bible; back to the experience of Jesus and the apostles; back to the richness of God's family tree of salvation and covenant experience; back to the faith once delivered to the saints. I stand ready to serve you and to help you recover all that God has for you.

In Messiah Jesus,

John D. Garr, Ph.D., Th.D.

Meet Dr. John Garr

Dr. John D. Garr is the founder and president of Restoration Foundation, an international, transdenominational, multi-ethnic networking organization– a coalition of scholars, church leaders, and laypersons who seek to restore the church to biblical Christianity by recovering and implementing the Hebrew foundations of Christian faith.

Dr. Garr's teaching ministry is unique in that it combines excellent scholarship with intense spirituality and personal integrity. He is a theologian with extensive and diversified training. At the same time, he is a minister with a history of more than forty years of wide-ranging service the international church. An academician with a pastor's heart, he is able to contextualize the great central truths of orthodox Christian faith in terms that laypersons can understand and incorporate into their lives. His ministry features teaching and preaching that challenges believers to faith that is manifest in a biblically sound, Christocentric lifestyle, grounded in the Hebraic heritage of Jesus and the apostles.

Dr. Garr's credentials include a Bachelors Degree in Theology, a Masters Degree in Theology (*summa cum laude*), a Doctor of Philosophy degree in Church Administration, and a Doctor of Theology degree from Evangelical Theological Seminary, where he now serves as professor of Biblical and Judaic Studies.

Having been called to Christian ministry at an early age, Dr. Garr has served the body of Christ in many ministerial capacities, including evangelist, pastor, overseer, presbyter, missionary, church planter, conference speaker, teacher, and seminary professor. In each of these capacities, he has served with integrity and distinction, applauded by both leaders and those whom he has served.

A prolific writer, Dr. Garr has authored many books, including most recently *Restoring Our Lost Legacy: Christianity's Hebrew Heritage*; *The Hem of His Garment: Touching the Power in God's Word*; *Living Emblems: Ancient Symbols of Faith*; *Christian Celebrations for Passover*; *God's Lamp, Man's Light: Mysteries of the Menorah*; and *Bless You!: Restoring the Biblically Hebraic Blessing*; and *Family Sanctuary: Restoring the Biblically Hebraic Home*. He is currently writing other books to chronicle both historically and theologically the emergence of Christianity from the matrix of Biblical Judaism, the subsequent Hellenization and Latinization of the church, the resultant Judaeophobia, anti-Judaism, and anti-Semitism that have characterized the church for nearly eighteen centuries, and the work of restoration that has been underway for the past five centuries to recover the church's biblical heritage. He serves as editor and publisher of *Restore!*, the official journal of Restoration Foundation. He has contributed hundreds of essays and theological studies to various magazines and journals.

For many years, Dr. Garr has cultivated his calling to promote unity in the international body of Christ. He offers the unique ability to create dialogue on polarized issues in theology and polity and to bring forth the consensus of a common ground upon which all can stand. He has extensive training and experience in facilitating dialogue. Through Restoration Foundation and other organizations, he promotes the biblical concept of unity in the pluriformity of diversity rather than the traditional concept of unity through uniformity and credalism. Dr. Garr teaches that believers can be united in central theology while having latitude and flexibility in the areas of peripheral theology.

Restoration Foundation, the educational organization that is a resource to the entire body of Christ, is one product and vehicle of Dr. Garr's ministry. The foundation was developed to meet the growing need in the international church for a forum that brings together scholars, church leaders, and laypersons for the purpose of analyzing the Jewish roots of Christian faith and to discover means of promoting and implementing the church's return to its biblical heritage. Dr. Garr believes that an over-Hellenized and over-Latinized church needs to recover its inherent Judaic ideals in order to be more Christian (in the sense of being more like Christ, her Jewish Lord) and in order to bring true maturity into the lives of believers.

Long an advocate of higher education that is focused in the Hebraic foundations of the Christian faith, Dr. Garr, in collaboration with scholars from around the world, has now launched Hebraic Heritage Christian School of Theology. A completely new concept in academia, this college will feature a curriculum developed around the historical and theological truths of Christianity's Jewish roots. It is the answer to growing world-wide demand for superior quality education that focuses on biblical truths and avoids centuries of Hellenist and Latin tradition that has severed most of the church from its Jewish roots. Dr. Garr serves as chancellor for the college.

Dr. Garr has made numerous visits to Israel, where he has interacted with the Christian and Jewish communities, building bridges of dialogue and communication. He is currently working with rabbis and scholars in Jerusalem, encouraging them to bring their understanding to Christians internationally so that the church can better understand Jews and Judaism and can collaborate in confronting the neo-Platonism, neo-paganism, and Eastern monism that are sweeping through Western society.

In order to further his vision for educating the body of Christ as to its Hebrew foundations, Dr. Garr is collaborating with various scholars and church leaders in seminars and symposiums throughout the world. He has taught these concepts on five continents and in over twenty nations to pastors, leaders, and scholars of over thirty denominations, including Anglicans and Presbyterians in India, Assemblies of God in Southern Africa, Presbyterians in West Africa, Methodists in Brazil, Pentecostal Holiness and Foursquare Gospel Churches in Argentina, and numerous denominations in Mexico. The teaching has been received with great acclaim because of the balanced biblicity that it features, its non-threatening style, and the absence of either legalism or antinomianism.

Dr. Garr has been married to the former Pat Hall (B.S. Business Administration, Covenant College) of Knoxville, Tennessee, for the past thirty-nine years. They have three sons, John David II (M.S. Mechanical Engineering, Tennessee Technological University, M.S. Environmental Engineering, University of Alabama, engineer and flight controller for NASA's Johnson Space Center in Houston, Texas), Timothy Daniel (B.S. Chemical Engineering, Tennessee Technological University, engineer and production specialist for Dow Chemical Company in Gales Ferry, Connecticut), and Stephen Michael (Pharm.D., University of the Sciences at Philadelphia, hospital pharmacist, Chaattanooga, Tennessee). They have three grandchildren, John III, Lillian, and Caleb. The Garrs reside in Atlanta, Georgia.

For complete information about the

Teaching, Equipping Ministry of Dr. John D. Garr,

Write:

Restoration Foundation

P.O. Box 421218

Atlanta, GA 30342

(678) 615-3568

(678) 357-7771

E-mail: info@restorationfoundation.org